THE P

~ You

ISBN-13: 978-1-4959-0702-9
ISBN-10: 1-4959-0702-3

Published by Springs International

DEDICATION

This book is dedicated to you and the fulfilment of your design-purpose in life.

CONTENTS

PREFACE

When purpose is unknown, abuse is inevitable
– Dr. Myles Munroe, OBE

What is the purpose of life? Do you know why you were born and why you are living? These are questions that you cannot afford to ignore. You cannot bury your head in the sand like the proverbial ostrich and assume that life is just about survival, work and pleasure. Is there more to life than all these? Have you any disappointment with the pressure of survival, the stress of work and the anti-climax of pleasure. Are you searching for meaning? Have you felt emptiness within? Do you struggle with sickness and disease? Are you lonely? Have you suffered losses? Why is life broken? Is there a God? Why are you here? How can you win? Is there more to life than all these? What is the purpose of life? The wiser you are, the more important the question becomes. This book will provide you the answers that you have been looking for. Your life will never remain the same!

CHAPTER 1
WHERE DO I COME FROM?

In order to understand the purpose of your life, one of the most important questions you will have to answer is 'Where do I come from?' This is because your understanding of your origin determines your perception of who you are and what you are living for.

Evolution vs. Creation:

There are two main world views on the origin of life: *Evolution* and *Creation*.

Evolution is the process by which different kinds of living organism are believed to have developed from earlier forms during the history of the earth through random mutations and natural selection.

Creation is the process by which the universe and all living organism are believed to have *come into instant existence by the command of a sovereign, supernatural and eternal spirit-being called God.*

Simply speaking, *evolution* claims that man developed from apes which in turn developed from reptiles which in turn developed from fishes which in turn developed from worms which in turn developed from sponges which in turn developed from single-cells which in turn developed from molecules and atoms through *random mutations* and *natural selection* over several billions of years.

Evolution by itself does not explain the origin of life. Therefore, the *evolution* theory which was proposed about 150 years ago has been combined with the *Big Bang* and *Abiogenesis* theories proposed thereafter, in order to explain how the entire world came into being.

Big Bang is the process by which the universe is believed to have been born by a sudden explosion. In a fraction of a second, the universe is believed to have grown from smaller than a single atom to bigger than a galaxy.

<u>Abiogenesis</u> is the process by which life is believed to have arisen spontaneously from the chemical evolution of non-living matter.

Big bang does not explain how the initial material and conditions that caused the *bang* came into being nor does it explain how an explosion can produce order without any form of intelligent intervention.

Abiogenesis has never been observed in any natural or artificial environment.

Since *evolution* claims to be a science, we expect it to be backed up by scientific evidence that validates it as being true. Therefore, it is important that we subject it to the scientific test and see what results we get.

Firstly, let us proceed with some basic definitions from the *Oxford dictionary*:

Fact: *a thing that is known or proved to be true.*

Hypothesis: *a supposition or proposed explanation made on the basis of limited evidence as a starting point for further investigation.*

Theory: *a supposition or a system of ideas intended to explain something, especially one based on general principles independent of the thing to be explained.*

Science: *the intellectual and practical activity encompassing the systematic study of the structure and behaviour of the physical and natural world through observation and experiment.*

Scientific method: *a method of procedure that has characterized natural science since the*

17th century, consisting in systematic observation, measurement, and experiment, and the formulation, testing, and modification of hypotheses.

Well now, *is every scientific theory* a *fact*? Of course not! A scientific theory becomes a fact when it has been proved to be consistently true with little margin of error. In order to analyse *evolution* in the light of true science, it is important to make a clear distinction between *evolution* and *natural selection*.

<u>Natural selection</u>: *the process whereby organisms better adapted to their environment tend to survive and produce more offspring.*

Natural selection, as verified by science, refers to the adaptation of different features of a specific life form to its environment. This is no new concept really as natural selection has been observed in varying degrees by the unlearned man throughout history. Natural selection is an horizontal change within the same life form. It is not a vertical change into higher life forms, for each life form can only select and adapt within its genetic pool.

Natural selection is not Evolution and Evolution is not Natural selection.

Testing Evolution:

1. Fossil record
The main scientific test of *evolution* is *the fossil test* proposed by its founder: Charles Darwin, who predicted the discovery of innumerable transitional life forms in the fossil record. Till date, despite 150 years of observation and millions of fossils, no transitional life form (supporting gradual evolution) has ever been found in the fossil record! The fossil record is now very extensive, yet all known animal body plans appear within it in the form they possess today. Furthermore, the structure of the fossil

record does not support the sequence of evolution suggested by the *evolution* theory.

Evolution has failed its own test, the fossil test laid down by its very own founder.

The fossil record also provides additional evidence that disagree with *evolution.* These include the discovery of human footprints alongside those of dinosaurs, primitive life forms at the beginning of the fossil record having very highly developed eyes and a purported 70-million year old tyrannosaurus fossil containing red blood cells and soft tissue!

Evolution is not a fact. It is a theory which has many gaping holes.

2. Eye Variety
Evolution has also failed *the eye test*. The greatest variety of eye design, not only in structure, but also in number and location, exists not among the vertebrates (e.g. apes

and humans) but among the so-called 'primitive' invertebrates (e.g. flies and insects). Moreover, advanced vision is found is more primitive animals. For example, most flies have hemispherical eyes which produce an image largely free of spherical distortion. The human eye can register up to 60 images per second while that of a lowly bee can do 300 images per second. For this reason, bees can see far better while rapidly moving.

The claims of Evolution have been severally disproven by scientific evidence.

3. Genetic Information
Another scientific test of *evolution* is *the genetic test* i.e. generation of new genetic information. How did worms produce new genetic information to develop fish fins, or fish produce new information to develop reptilian legs? Advances in technology allow scientist to rapidly and intelligently make genes duplicate, and yet still, there has been no evidence of new functions in the gene.

Most mutations result in functional losses, abnormalities, or no change at all.

Evolution is an unscientific ideology, propagated and asserted by atheistic scientists.

A major source of confusion that makes some people gravitate towards believing in the unscientific evolution theory is the issue of *radiometric dating* into the past.

Radiometric dating is a measurement technique used to date materials such as rocks, usually based on a comparison between the observed abundance of a naturally occurring radioactive isotope and its decay products, using known decay rates.

All *radiometric dating* methods were developed after the evolution theory was proposed and are based on at least three fundamental assumptions:

1. The original conditions are known.

2. The process is unaltered by external forces or contamination.
3. The decay rate is constant.

If any measurement is based on an assumption, then that assumption must be confirmed and validated as *factual* for that measurement to be accurate.
Example: A meter rule can only give a good measurement of length if it lacks the capacity to shrink or expand with time.

The first assumption of *radiometric dating* into the past is speculative. Is there an *accurate* record of the radio-isotope state beyond recorded history? Is there even an *accurate* record of the radio-isotope state just before radiometric dating was invented?

The second assumption of *radiometric dating* cannot be guaranteed because dating samples are subject to heat and water contamination and this applies more predominantly to samples from the past. In fact, *radiometric dating* is known to produce grossly inaccurate results when heat contamination is involved in the process as is the case with many volcanic rocks. For example, eruptions from the Hawaiian volcanoes which occurred in the year 1800 were dated in the range of millions and billions of years.

A scientific measurement system must be based on facts, measurements and mathematics. It cannot accommodate unproven assumptions.

The failure of the fundamental assumptions of *radiometric dating into the past* explains why its results are *geometrically misleading*. It is therefore no wonder that dinosaur bones dated as 70 million years old were found to contain red blood cells and soft tissue which should have decomposed completely within thousands of years. As it is, evolution scientists who hold on to the reliability of *radiometric dating* into the past, do so to justify their beliefs rather than science. It should be noted that radiometric dating results are always being subjected to tremendous tweaking in many instances, in order to conform to evolutionist belief.

Radiometric dating into the past is grossly inaccurate due to its unproven assumptions.

The failure to scientifically prove *abiogenesis* till date supports the overwhelming evidence that life cannot come from non-living or natural sources. Furthermore, there is so much intelligent complexity in the universe and even in the basic cells of all living things. This ultimately implies that life originated from a supernatural source that is more intelligent and more powerful than the whole of nature itself. Scientists refer to this concept as *intelligent design*.

Intelligent Design: *the theory that life, or the universe, cannot have arisen by chance and was designed and created by some intelligent entity.*

The fact that professional scientists and researchers exist today clearly attests to the depths of information complexity involved in various fields of enquiry that have yet to be unravelled. To attribute all these intelligence to randomness and chance is very absurd.

Evolutionist set out to disprove the existence of God, but they have only come up with a new god: Randomness + mutations + chance.

Having shown that *evolution* is both unscientific and absurd, we will now proceed to look at *creation*.

If evolution be true, then man is a product of chance, and his life is ultimately meaningless.

Creation is the process by which the universe and all living organism are believed to have come into instant existence by the command of a sovereign, supernatural and eternal spirit-being called God.

In the beginning (time) **God created the heavens** (space) **and the earth** (matter).
– Genesis 1:1

Simply speaking, *creation* says that the whole universe and all life forms (plants, fishes, birds, reptiles, dinosaurs, apes, man etc.) were specifically created by command of God in a particular order at a specific time period. According to the Bible, God created time, space and matter. In this regard, all of creation comes from the same source. Is it any wonder then that similarities are found between different life forms?

In the beginning was the Word, and the Word was with God, and the Word was God.
He was in the beginning with God.
All things were made through Him, and without Him nothing was made that was made.
– John 1:1-3

According to the Bible, God created the heavens and the earth by His eternal Word. He commanded the clouds, sky, atmosphere, sea, land, sun, moon, stars, sea creatures, birds, and land animals into existence by His Word of faith. Then God formed man, the climax of all creation, from the elements of the earth and breathed spirit into Him and man became a living soul.

Is creation possible? Well now, if God by definition is a sovereign, supernatural and eternal spirit-being, *creation* must be really easy for Him since He possesses infinite power. In this regard, it is very important to note that God does not need a *cruel* evolutionary process to create man.

Did creation really happen? Let us consider some of the evidence and see if *creation* is really for the thinking man.

Testing Creation:

1. Information science
Entropy (disorder, noise, randomness) is the exact opposite of *Information* (order, signal, design). Naturally speaking, information

(order) always degrades towards entropy (disorder). Disorder cannot transform into order without intelligent intervention. The second law of thermodynamics implies that the universe started in a state of order (thereby supporting *creation*) and will end in maximum disorder. Every mutation involves the loss of information, not generation of new information. Intelligent products such as cars, aeroplanes, skyscrapers, cruise ships and space ships do not just happen. They all require a skilful and intelligent designer (inventor or creator). Therefore, *information science* shows us that the universe and all life must have been designed and created.

2. Cell complexity

The 'simple' *cell* of any living organism possesses immense *complexity* and design. This includes memory, processing units, transport, secure communications, quality control and repair mechanisms. Consider the information content of the DNA and its replication process. Haemoglobin is the oxygen-transporting protein in the red blood cells of all vertebrates. An Haemoglobin molecule consists of 574 amino acids i.e. 574 elements from an alphabet of 20. There are 20^{574} permutations possible but only one of them is Haemoglobin. This implies an incredibly skilful design. The probability of Haemoglobin being formed by chance is 1 in 10^{650}. This means one chance in a billion billion billion billion billion billion billion billion … (up to 72 multiples). This chance is not only technically absurd, it is practically impossible i.e. an absolutely outstanding miracle that supports *creation*. It is clear that God has embedded His creative signature right into the simple cell. The cell is shown to be more intelligent than advanced man-made devices in our world today.

For since the creation of the world His invisible attributes are clearly seen, being understood by the things that are made, even His eternal power and Godhead, so that they are without excuse.
– Romans 1:20

3. Astronomy and cosmology

Consider the expanding universe with its billions of galaxies, the milky way galaxy with its billions of stars in their constellations, the enormous energy of the sun, the revolving planets in the solar system and their moons, the daily rotation of the earth, monthly revolution of the moon around the earth and the yearly revolution of the earth around the sun. The planet earth is specifically designed for life and its location from the sun is just about right. Consider also that all of these bodies are constantly in motion and are suspended in 'empty' Space. Could this 'immense, advanced and orderly' Space have resulted from explosions, randomness, time and chance, without any form of intelligent intervention? Not likely at all!

The *big bang* theory which is based on the observation of an expanding universe actually supports *creation* in that it states that the universe had a beginning and did not always exist. Furthermore, its claim that the universe developed from nothing into a galaxy in less than a second is an absolutely outstanding miracle that supports a supernatural *creation*.

The heavens declare the glory of God;
And the firmament shows His handiwork.
Day unto day utters speech,
And night unto night reveals knowledge.
There is no speech nor language
where their voice is not heard.
– Psalm 19:1-3

4. Historical records

How far back do the *historical records* go? The earliest actual recorded date in human history (Egyptian records) is not earlier than 1900B.C. Furthermore, historians claim that recorded human history goes back to about only 5,000 years. This evidence agrees with the Biblical account of *creation* rather than that of evolution which claims that man has been around for about a million years and stopped evolving about 100,000 years ago. If *creation* were not true, wouldn't it be odd that although man stopped evolving 100,000 years ago, civilization suddenly exploded into intense activity only about 5,000 years ago.

5. *Man's superiority*

Man is not just another animal. Man's level of overall sophistication is *highly superior* to that of any other animal. Man is in a special class with his mental capability which results in skills such as language, writing, math, science, technology, literature, art and music. Man's superiority has changed all of history through agriculture, architecture, engineering and medicine. Above all of this is the fact that man uniquely possesses a spiritual (subconscious, inner, heart) nature that has resulted in diverse kinds of religions or ideologies throughout all of history. An overflow of this spiritual nature is his moral nature (a sense of right and wrong) that has resulted in diverse kinds of social, legal and political systems throughout all of history.

Then God said, "Let Us make man in Our image, according to Our likeness; let them have

dominion over the fish of the sea, over the birds of the air, and over the cattle, over all the earth and over every creeping thing that creeps on the earth – Genesis 1:26

Men have used their understanding of the laws of nature to achieve technological wonders. Men have also used their understanding of spiritual laws to achieve supernatural wonders. All these observations agree with the account of *creation* which says that man was created in his own special class, in the very image of God. To assert that man evolved is to demean his essential worth.

When I consider Your heavens, the work of Your fingers, The moon and the stars, which You have ordained, What is man that You are mindful of him, And the son of man that You visit him? For You have made him a little lower than the angels, And You have crowned him with glory and honour. You have made him to have dominion over the works of Your hands; You have put all things under his feet.
– Psalm 8:3-6

CHAPTER 2
WHO IS GOD?

Now that we understand that the universe and all life originated from God through the process of *creation*, the next question we have to consider is who God is. For if we don't understand the attributes of our maker, it is impossible to fully understand why he made us. No designer spends time to develop a highly intelligent product for no tangible reason. In creating us, God must have a desire that needs fulfilment through us.

Attributes of the Most High:

1. God is Life Infinite
The Most High is the source of life. The fullness of life and vitality flows forth from Him. God is full of infinite transcendent life. He is infinite in wisdom and power. He is the sovereign supernatural and eternal Spirit-being who created the heavens and the earth.

He has no beginning and no end. He is perfect, immortal, invincible and immutable. He is omnipotent, omnipresent and omniscient. He sets the laws of nature and of the spirit. He determines the moral standard. God is Spirit and can only be contacted spiritually. In this regard, it is important to note that the Most High is infinitely above all, the only true God.

**All things were made through Him, and without Him nothing was made that was made.
In Him was life, and the life was the light of men.**
– John 1:3-4

2. God is Light
The Most High is Light and there exists no darkness in Him. Light brings development. God is totally good and there exists no badness in Him. He is the embodiment of all things good. The existence of all creation depends on His goodness. It is His goodness that holds the heavens and the earth in empty space and it is His goodness that provides us

the sun that shines on the earth, the rain that waters the earth and the fresh air that supports respiration and agriculture.

> **This is the message which we have heard from Him and declare to you, that God is light and in Him is no darkness at all.**
> − 1 John 1:5

3. God is visional and missional

The Most High has not created the universe and life just for the fun of it. God's vision is based on his purpose called *Worship* and God's mission is based on His plan called *History*. God's purpose necessitates *creation* and *free will* while his plan necessitates 'the beginning and the end' of all things. God planned the ages long before he created them and the whole of history is 'His story'.

> **… For it is written, 'You shall worship the LORD your God, and Him only you shall serve.'**
> − Luke 4:8
> **… For at the appointed time the end shall be.**
> − Daniel 8:19

4. God is a relationship

The Most High is one God, revealed in three perfectly united persons: The eternal Father, His eternal Word and His eternal Spirit. We can easily understand this when we understand that the word of a man represents that man and the spirit of a man also represents that man. God is a triune being just as man is triune (i.e. spirit, soul and body). 3 is the number of divine completeness, which is also reflected in the 3 qualities of the universe (time, space and matter), 3 qualities of time (past, present and future), 3 qualities of space (length, width and height) and 3 qualities of matter (solid, liquid and gas).

For there are three that bear witness in heaven: the Father, the Word, and the Holy Spirit; and these three are one.
— 1 John 5:7

5. God is relational

The Most High is neither disconnected from nor disinterested in His creation. God is a father to all of His creation. Man is His supreme project. He made man, is mindful of man, seeks man out, seeks to relate with man and has set eternity (the need of knowing Him) in the heart of every man. His relationship with man is fundamental to His purpose and plan.

> **What is man that You are mindful of him,**
> **And the son of man that You visit him?**
> – Psalm 8:4

6. God is Faithful

The Most High is a faith God. He operates by faith because He has bound Himself to His Word. He calls Himself by the name: 'I AM WHO I AM'. God cannot lie; He is always faithful and true to His Word. Faith pleases Him and He rewards faith and obedience. He rewards those who diligently seek Him. Therefore, from the point of view of man's relationship with God, faith is the most fundamental spiritual principle. Faith means complete trust in God and His Word.

**But without faith it is impossible to please Him,
for he who comes to God must believe that He is,
and that He is a rewarder of those who diligently
seek Him.** – Hebrews 11:6

7. God is Righteous and Holy
The Most High is Righteous. He defines Truth
by His Word and always does what is
absolutely right. God is Holy. He is full of
perfection and sinless purity. God is thrice
holy. He is infinitely pure, infinitely beautiful
and infinitely glorious. He is altogether lovely
and altogether worthy. He is distinct, separate
and in a class by Himself. He is stainless. All
His attributes are holy. His love is holy, His
mercy is holy and His justice is holy. He cannot
break His moral standard and He does not
condone sin, whether by angels or humans.

**No one is holy like the LORD,
For there is none besides You,
Nor is there any rock like our God.**
– 1 Samuel 2:2

8. God is Love

The Most High is loving because that is His nature. His love is compassion, not emotion. His love is never discriminatory. God loves you and cares about you, irrespective of your background. He understands you beyond all others. He loves you because He made you and always desires the very best for you. God is gracious, benevolent and full of kindness. He acts to save. It was God's Love that necessitated the incarnation of the *eternal Word*. He literally came 'down to earth' to sacrifice Himself, in order to pay the universal and eternal price for Sin.

For God so loved the world that He gave His only begotten Son, that whoever believes in Him should not perish but have everlasting life.
– John 3:16

9. God is patient and merciful

The Most High is patient with the sinner, forgives the repentant and also provides a way of escape from judgement. He causes His sun to shine on the good and the evil. He provides fresh air for the just and the unjust. His mercies are new every morning. However, God's mercy is His prerogative and cannot be taken for granted. God cannot break His Word and He cannot bless disobedience. Time will ultimately run out for those who persistently refuse to take advantage of God's mercy.

**The LORD is gracious and full of compassion,
Slow to anger and great in mercy.**
– Psalm 145:8

10. God is Just

The Most High is Just and He is eternally committed to justice. The judgements of God during our life on earth are temporal, an extension of His mercy, in order to bring us to repentance and blessing. The judgements of God when we pass on from this life are final and eternal. Every man will be judged according to how they lived on earth with respect to the purpose of God. Their eternal place is determined by their faith in response to God's Love and their eternal state is determined by their works in response to God's Word. The justice of God glorifies His holiness and the glory of God is the greatest goal of all existence. Therefore, in all of eternity, God must continuously be glorified.

> **"You are worthy, O Lord,**
> **To receive glory and honour and power;**
> **For You created all things,**
> **And by Your will they exist and were created."**
> – Revelation 4:11

The Most High reflected:

Notice that all the attributes of the Most High are relevant to man. Man mirrors and shadows the Most High. He desires power and dominion. He resists defeat and seeks to rule over his world. He fights wars in order to preserve his freedom. He desires light and development. He makes inventions and works hard to improve his quality of life. He makes definite plans based on definite purposes and has the innate capacity to envision and do great things. He desires social relationships as reflected in family, friends, tribes and nations. Man desires moral uprightness, cleanliness, beauty and glory as reflected in character references, reward systems, hygiene ratings, fashion, cosmetics, lights and fireworks. Man desires to love and be loved. He desires forgiveness and mercy as reflected in official pardons and royal prerogatives of mercy. Man desires a just, fair and smooth-running society. Therefore men make laws to govern, expect compliance and apply corresponding punishment to offenders. It is even asserted that ignorance is not an excuse in law.

Who is like You, O LORD, among the gods?
Who is like You, glorious in holiness,
Fearful in praises, doing wonders?
– Exodus 15:11

The Most High revealed:

Because God is Spirit, it is important to understand that the spiritual world is the real world and the physical world is only a subset of it. The things that are visible are made from things not visible and the spiritual realm is much wider, longer, deeper and higher than the physical.

For since the creation of the world His invisible attributes are clearly seen, being understood by the things that are made, even His eternal power and Godhead, so that they are without excuse.
– Romans 1:20

Now, given all the attributes of the Most High, it is clear that finite man cannot define infinite God. Therefore, God must reveal Himself to His supreme creation (man) in a most definite, comprehensive and consistent way. Certainly yes, since the definite revelation of God is most imperative for the development of a true relationship between God and man, in order to fulfil the eternal purpose of God. This is exactly what the Most High God has done through the ages by speaking His Word through His *prophets* and *apostles*.

All Scripture is given by inspiration of God, and is profitable for doctrine, for reproof, for correction, for instruction in righteousness, that the man of God may be complete, thoroughly equipped for every good work.
– 2 Timothy 3:16-17

The *Bible* is the most definite, comprehensive and consistent revelation of the Most High. It is the Spirit-inspired Word of God to you. It is the user manual of life. It has been carefully compiled and accurately preserved by the Most High, so that you can have unlimited access to knowing Him, because knowing your creator is the beginning of the fulfilment of your design-purpose in life.

The Bible is the most printed and most distributed book of all time.

The Bible accurately foretells many specific events in detail, years, decades and centuries before they occur. Till date, about 2000 Bible prophecies have been fulfilled to the letter, and the remaining 500 prophecies about the end of time are unfolding progressively. The Bible records the very beginning of time in detail and foretells the very end of time in detail. The scientific accuracy of the Bible is outstanding, for it reveals numerous scientific facts, long before they were ever discovered or confirmed by science. These include verses revealing a spherical, rotating and suspended earth, innumerable stars, ocean currents, ocean-floor mountains and medical hygiene.

The Bible contains the mind of God, the state of man, the way of salvation, the doom of sinners, and the happiness of believers. Its doctrines are holy, its precepts are binding, its histories are true, and its decisions are immutable.
Read it to be wise, believe it to be safe, and practice it to be holy.
– Gideon's International

CHAPTER 3
WHY AM I HERE?

The Composition of Man:

In order to fully understand the purpose of man, we need to understand his composition. Man is a triune being, made up of spirit, soul and body. In fact, man is a spirit, has a soul and lives in a body. With your spirit, you contact the spiritual realm. With your soul, you contact the intellectual realm (your soul consists of your mind, will and emotion). With your body, you contact the physical realm. Your spirit is the core you, your heart, your subconscious, your inner self and the very centre of your being.

And the LORD God formed man of the dust of the ground (body)**, and breathed into his nostrils the breath of life** (spirit)**; and man became a living being** (soul)**.** – Genesis 2:7

The Purpose of Man:

As explained in the previous chapter, God's vision is based on His purpose called *Worship*. He desires worship and totally deserves it. God's purpose necessitated *creation* and *free will.* The greatest asset that God has given to every man is free will: the ability to make choices. Your will emanates from your spirit and is enacted in your soul. God wants you to use that free will to choose Him and worship Him. Indeed, worship cannot be genuine if it is not freely given. God wants you to know Him intimately, love Him deeply, honour Him reverently, praise Him abundantly, serve Him faithfully, glorify Him continuously and enjoy Him totally. Essentially, God wants you to live in Him and for Him, because you come from Him. *Your design-purpose is to worship God.*

> *The design-purpose of every man's life is to worship (know, love, honour, praise, serve, glorify and enjoy) God forever.*

Worship is a relationship of the highest order and deepest kind between a creature (man) and his creator (God). Worship is a lifestyle and not just about occasional acts or ceremonies. Worship involves attention and dedication. Worship is of the heart, the very centre of a man's being and it involves the totality of a man's daily living.

Worship is the expression of reverence, adoration, and devotion to an entity

What is the object of your worship? What do you care most about? What receives predominant attention in your life? What are you devoted to? What are you living for? What makes you tick? Is it money, affluence or fortune? Is it fame, recognition, reputation or status? Is it partner, family or friends? Is it leisure, pleasure or comfort? Is it refreshment or entertainment? Is it gadgets, adventure, competition, sports or games? Is it power or influence? Is it beauty, fitness, attention or acceptance? Is it education, career or work?

Are you living for the Most High, the only one who is eternally worthy? Are you living for Him daily? Is God the object of your worship?

... The LORD our God, the LORD is one! You shall love the LORD your God with all your heart, with all your soul, and with all your strength.
– Deuteronomy 6:4-5

No designer spends time to develop a highly intelligent product for no tangible reason. Remember that you did not make yourself. *Your design-purpose is what you were made for. Your design-purpose is why you are here.* In creating us, God has a desire that needs fulfilment through us and that desire is *worship* (knowing God, walking with Him and living for Him). Are you fulfilling your design-purpose or are you chasing only self-centred purposes? *True fulfilment in life can only be achieved by being all you were made to be.*

The greatest pursuit in life is knowing God and walking with Him.

High Treason:

In most countries of the world, (high) treason is considered as a most severe offence. In the United Kingdom for example, the crime of high treason carried a maximum penalty of death until 1998, when the penalty was reduced to life imprisonment.

Treason: the crime of betraying one's country, especially by attempting to kill or overthrow the sovereign or government.

Why is treason considered as so great an offence? Well, your country provides you with the security that enables you to have a living. Therefore, treason is seen as a betrayal of the state. However, it is important to realise that you are not just a citizen of your country but also a part of God's creation and therefore under the Kingdom of the Most High.

You shall have no other gods before Me.
– Exodus 20:3

God expects you to make use of your free will to freely choose to worship Him. *True and genuine worship is that which is given freely in the acknowledgement of who God is*. The question is not why you should worship God. The question is why not? God is your creator and sustains your existence after all. He provides the air that you breathe. Every good and perfect gift comes from God who holds all things together. Therefore you do not have any tangible excuse not to worship God because you owe all of your existence to Him.

Idolatry is to disregard the Most High as the only true God and/or to worship any other entity (including self-worship) in partial or full substitution of Him.

In this regard, Sin can be essentially defined as rebellion against the Most High. The worst form of idolatry is the worship of self and selfishness is at the root of every sin. The antidote to all sin is repentance and it is as free as your 'free will'.

Sin is rebellion against the Most High and the antidote to sin is repentance.

God is patient with the sinner, forgives the repentant and also provides a way of escape from judgement. However, time will ultimately run out for those who persistently refuse to take advantage of God's mercy.

God is Spirit, and those who worship Him must worship in spirit and truth.
– John 4:24

God is seeking for *true worshippers* (John 4:23-24): those who will worship Him in spirit (with all their heart) and in truth (without hypocrisy). There is no higher calling and no greater honour than to worship the Most High, for He made us all and He alone deserves all the glory, now and forevermore.

For of Him and through Him and to Him are all things, to whom be glory forever. Amen.
– Romans 11:36

CHAPTER 4
WHY IS LIFE BROKEN?

The Origin of Evil:

When the Most High created the heavens and the earth, He also created the angels (free-willed spirit-beings, also called 'sons of God' and 'morning stars') to behold His glory and minister to His divine purpose. Everything was perfect, for God is light and in Him is no darkness at all. There were archangels set above the angelic race such as Lucifer, Michael and Gabriel. Lucifer was the top archangel, the anointed cherub, full of excellent beauty and made as an embodiment of excellent worship.

**You were the anointed cherub who covers;
I established you; You were on the holy
mountain of God; … You were perfect in your
ways from the day you were created,
Till iniquity was found in you.**
– Ezekiel 28:14-15

However, Lucifer became proud and vain in his imaginations, and thought that he could *evolve* and become like the Most High. He failed the necessary test of obedience and rebelled against God. Lucifer wanted and sought to be worshipped! He succeeded in deceiving one third of the angels and sought to usurp the throne of God.

Your heart was lifted up because of your beauty;
You corrupted your wisdom ...
– Ezekiel 28:17

The *high treason* committed by Lucifer and his cohorts gave rise to the first judgement: *Darkness (spiritual death)*. By definition, darkness is the absence of light. Spiritual darkness simply means spiritual separation from God: the source of life and light. It means alienation from the God-kind of life. It is the root cause of death, decay and all evil. Darkness is the righteous initial judgement for Sin (i.e. rebellion against the Most High), for it is an excusal from the goodness of Heaven.

Lucifer had no valid excuse for his rebellion (disobedience), for he had beheld and experienced the fullness of God's glory. Therefore, he was eternally demoted from his original status and his eternal destiny was sealed forever. The pride of Lucifer ultimately led to his fall. Therefore, he lost his beauty and glory, became the father of darkness (death, decay and all evil) and his name was changed to Satan.

> **"How you are fallen from heaven,**
> **O Lucifer, son of the morning!**
> **How you are cut down to the ground,**
> **You who weakened the nations!**
> – Isaiah 14:12

Satan is also known as the devil, the red dragon (fiery dinosaur), old twisted serpent, leviathan (sea monster), the prince of the power of the air, the prince of this world and the god of this age. The angels that fell with him became forces of evil such as demons, devils, evil spirits, principalities, powers, rulers of the darkness of this world (deities and gods) and spiritual wickedness in high places (wicked territorial spirits). Their final judgement is in the lake of fire and brimstone but this has been delayed in order to serve God's purpose of shaming them.

Darkness (spiritual death) is the initial judgement for rebellion against the Most High

The Fall of Man:

When Satan and his cohorts fell, they were cast away from God's throne to the earth and space. The effects of the fall began to have a negative impact on the world. Therefore the earth became formless and empty, and darkness covered the deep, but the Spirit of God was hovering over the surface of the waters. Then God said: "Let there be light" and there was light. And God separated the light from the darkness. Consequently, God embarked on recreating the earth, thereby getting it ready for His supreme project: Man.

So God created man in His own image; in the image of God He created him; male and female He created them.
– Genesis 1:27

God commanded the earth to bring forth plants and animals and it did. However, when it came to man, God took time to form his body from the earth and then breathed spirit into him. For this reason, the first man, Adam, is also called a 'son of God', just like the angels. Adam was the representative head of the human race and the first command God gave to Adam and his wife: Eve, was to dominate the earth, enjoy it and subdue it. Mankind was created to put Satan under total control in the earth. Satan is no adversary for God for he can't match God in any way. Rather, Satan is the adversary of mankind because man was created as his nemesis, to bring Satan to shame and humiliation.

Then God blessed them, and God said to them, "Be fruitful and multiply; fill the earth and subdue it; have dominion over the fish of the sea, over the birds of the air, and over every living thing that moves on the earth." – Genesis 1:28

Before the fall, Adam had a vital relationship with God and spent time in communion with the Most High. Adam was a supernatural sinless son of God who had all the freedom he needed to administer and enjoy the earth. However, in consistency with God's eternal purpose, it was necessary to test the obedience (allegiance) of man to God. And so, Adam was supremely commanded not to eat of the tree of the knowledge of good and evil. However, Satan, also known as the tempter, took the form of a cunning serpent and tempted Eve by introducing *doubt and lies*.

And the LORD God commanded the man, saying, "Of every tree of the garden you may freely eat; but of the tree of the knowledge of good and evil you shall not eat, for in the day that you eat of it you shall surely die." – Genesis 2:16-17

Eve was deceived into thinking that God lied and did not have their best interests at heart. Eve was deceived into thinking she could be a *god* on her own right (independent, wise and *evolved*, with no need for the Most High). Consequently, Eve and Adam committed *high treason* by disobeying God's supreme command, thereby breaking their allegiance to the Most High.

God cannot lie. He is always faithful to His Word.

It is important to note that both Adam and Eve had the full capacity to obey God's command; otherwise God would have been unfair, which He cannot be, for God is *Just*. Their disobedience was a product of their own bad choice. If they had passed the supreme test (probation) set by God, they would have partaken of *the tree of life* and confirmed their sinless supernatural status forever!

The devil is the father of lies. His derives his power over men from lies and deception.

God's sovereignty sets the boundaries and general principles;
Man's free will determines the course (path).

Consequences of the Fall:

Through the disobedience of the first man, Adam, all generations of men became subject to spiritual death (and as a result, physical death). For in the very moment that Adam sinned, he died spiritually and lost his vital relationship with God. However, despite *the fall*, the residue of *life infinite* in Adam was still so much that he lived for almost 1,000 years. Even so, he never lived forever as he could have, but died at 930 years old, still within one historical day of 1,000 years.

But, beloved, do not forget this one thing, that with the Lord one day is as a thousand years, and a thousand years as one day.
– 2 Peter 3:8

Adam, the first man, was given the title-deed of the earth, but he lost this to Satan when he sinned, thereby crowning the devil as *the god of this world system*. God cannot rule directly on the earth until the lease He gave to man (i.e. 6 days of creation = 6,000 years of man's rule, for 6 is the number of man) runs out. Till then, God's rule in the earth will always require the cooperation of mankind. Man is therefore vital to God's interventions.

For in six days the LORD made the heavens and the earth, the sea, and all that is in them, and rested the seventh day. Therefore the LORD blessed the Sabbath day and hallowed it.
– Exodus 20:11

Adam lost his dominion with the resultant effect that darkness (spiritual death) started to reign in the earth. All of creation has been subjected to a bondage to decay and corruption. *This explains why life is broken*. For out of darkness comes decay, deformities, disease, defeat, destruction, disorder and death. Plants and animals (including the micro-organisms that cause sickness and disease) became wild in varying degrees. Man ultimately became a flesh-eater and his life-span shortened progressively from about 1,000 years after the fall to about 100 years today. But God will always make a way, even when there seems to be no way.

> **Behold, I will do a new thing,**
> **Now it shall spring forth;**
> **Shall you not know it?**
> **I will even make a road in the wilderness**
> **And rivers in the desert.**
> – Isaiah 43:19

Notice that Satan could not rule on the earth until he got man to cooperate with him in disobedience and rebellion against God. So also, God cannot rule on the earth until He gets man to cooperate with him in *faith and obedience*. Through the disobedience of the first man: Adam, the earth and its inhabitants became subject to the power of death and the bondage to decay. This explains the scientific Law of Entropy. Man lost his dominion to his adversary, the devil, who then became the god (ruler) of this world system. However, God is never to be beaten, for He is always one step ahead!

Every human is born with a fallen, sinful nature.

Freedom and Bondage:

Freedom is defined as the power or right to act, speak, or think as one wants. However, true freedom can only be guaranteed by order. Imagine what it will be like for several cars to drive on the highway without any traffic rules. That would be disaster! Freedom can only be guaranteed by appropriate moral boundaries; otherwise it will lead to chaos. This is why *free* societies must be governed by the rule of law. Limitless freedom always leads to bondage. *God is the limitless Limit that guarantees true freedom*. This is because

He is the most worthy person to define the moral standard, since He is the Most High who is *Just* and possesses *Infinite Wisdom*.

Freedom can only be guaranteed by appropriate moral boundaries; otherwise it will lead to chaos.

Have you ever wondered why you have to go through tests and exams, before degrees and certificates are awarded. Why do employees have to go through a probationary period before their employment status is confirmed? A successful probation (test, exam) leads to confirmation (validation, certification). This reflects how God deals with men and angels.

Performance must be tested
before rewards are confirmed.

Lucifer failed his supreme test and is damned forever. He had no excuse, for he had beheld and experienced the fullness of God's glory. Adam and Eve also failed their supreme test, due to the deception from Satan, but God in

His mercy had foreseen this and also provided a way out to save and restore mankind.

Through the LORD's mercies we are not consumed, Because His compassions fail not. They are new every morning; Great is Your faithfulness.
– Lamentations 3:22-23

So we see that the only way for man to walk with God and to experience true freedom is to 'trust and obey'. However, a life of obedience cannot be achieved without an attitude of humility. *Obedience and humility go together*.

Obedience is the greatest human responsibility.

It was *pride* that led to the fall of Satan and it can be rightly said that pride is the greatest sin ever, for it leads to deliberate rebellion against the Most High. God resists the proud but gives grace to the humble. *The antidote to pride is quick repentance and a consistent attitude of submission towards to God*.

Pride is the greatest sin ever, for it leads to deliberate rebellion against the Most High.

History: The Plan of Redemption:

Although man fell, God always had something better in mind: *Redemption*. God's plan from the foundations of the world had always been to redeem man so that he can fulfil his design-purpose (worship) to the open shame of Satan. And so in pronouncing judgement upon the serpent (Satan) for tempting Eve, God introduces the *Seed of the Woman*, thereby foretelling *the eternal sacrifice* of Christ who was born of a virgin, an outstanding historical event that happened about 4,000 years later.

And I will put enmity
Between you and the woman,
And between your seed and her Seed;
He shall bruise your head,
And you shall bruise His heel.
– Genesis 3:15

Furthermore, the Most High introduced the concept of redemption by *blood sacrifice*. He started this off by shedding the first animal blood in order to provide clothes made of animal skin for Adam and Eve. The sacrificial shedding of pure animal blood represents *atonement*: one life given for another.

And according to the law almost all things are purified with blood, and without shedding of blood there is no remission. – Hebrews 9:22

However, the blood of *pure unblemished* animals can only atone for sins temporarily, but could not take away the human sin problem. Therefore, a supernatural lamb was needed for eternal redemption.

... as of a lamb without blemish and without spot. He indeed was foreordained before the foundation of the world, but was manifest in these last times for you
– 1 Peter 1:19-20

God also instituted several covenants (i.e. Adamic, Noahic, Abrahamic, Mosaic and Davidic covenants) as a basis for His continuous relationship with man through the ages, and to grant special blessings to mankind, all leading up to the climax, i.e. the final *new covenant*, which is enacted by the blood of the promised redeemer, the lamb set apart from the foundations of the world.

For it is not possible that the blood of bulls and goats could take away sins.
– Hebrews 10:4

Isn't it amazing that the plan of *redemption* is even coded in the names of the *Messianic Seed-line* from the fall to the flood, i.e. Adam to Noah, for the names 'Adam – Seth – Enosh – Kenan – Mahalalel – Jared – Enoch – Methuselah – Lamech – Noah' mean *'Man – appointed – mortal – sorrow. – Blessed God – come down – teaching. – His death shall bring – the despairing – rest and comfort'*.

Have you not known? Have you not heard?
The everlasting God, the LORD,
The Creator of the ends of the earth,
Neither faints nor is weary.
His understanding is unsearchable.
– Isaiah 40:28

Further Study:

1.   Job 38:4-7
2.   Psalm 103:20
3.   Revelation 12:3-4
4.   Ezekiel 28:11-19
5.   Isaiah 14:12-21
6.   Ephesians 2:2
7.   2 Corinthians 4:4
8.   Ephesians 6:12
9.   Colossians 2:15
10.   Isaiah 27:1
11.   Romans 5:12
12.   Romans 3:23
13.   Romans 6:23
14.   Proverbs 9:10
15.   James 4:6-10
16.   Genesis 3:21
17.   Hebrews 9:22
18.   Genesis 5

CHAPTER 5
HOW CAN I WIN?

The Incarnation:

Universal man hates defeat and bondage. There is an innate desire in the heart of every person for victory and success. The universal cry of man is for the restoration of lost dominion. Man wants to conquer darkness and death. He wants to prevail over sickness, disease, poverty, disaster and disorder. This universal cry of man has resulted in various traditions and religions all over the world. Religion is man seeking God. However, the Most High has already taken the initiative to answer the universal cry since the very foundations of the world, long before the fall of Adam and Eve. And the answer to this cry involved the incarnation of the Most High (Himself) in human form. Literally speaking, God 'came down to earth' to redeem man, for only God could do it. *The eternal Word*, the second person of the triune God, took on human form in the person of *Jesus Christ* (*Yeshua Mashiach*, in Hebrew) about 2,014 years ago. The name 'Jesus' means '*The Lord who saves*' and 'Christ' means '*the anointed one and His anointing*'. He came to save us!

And the Word became flesh and dwelt among us, and we beheld His glory, the glory as of the only begotten of the Father, full of grace and truth.
– John 1:14

Jesus Christ is the divine-human, the God-man, fully God and fully man. He is *the Seed of the Woman*, for He was born of a virgin, through the supernatural work of the Holy Spirit. *The eternal Word* was not born of any earthly father, for it was *the Heavenly Father* who superintended His incarnation, and this is why Jesus Christ is called *the Son of God*. The eternal Word had to come down as a man, to do what man could not do, in order to redeem man from spiritual death, defeat and bondage. He didn't have to do it, but it was His love (compassion) that motivated Him.

**Therefore the Lord Himself will give you a sign:
Behold, the virgin shall conceive and bear a Son,
and shall call His name Immanuel.**
– Isaiah 7:14

It's all about Him:

The whole of history is all about Him. All the
sixty-six books of the Bible speak about Him.
The Law and the prophets spoke about Him.
All things were made by Him and for Him. He
existed before anything else and He is the one
who holds all things together. Let us consider
the historical record in the book of Genesis for
example. In the creation, He is the Word that
created all things, the Light that stepped
down into darkness, the Sun of Righteousness
that sustains all life, the bright Morning Star,
the second man and last Adam: incarnated as
the express image of God, the head of all
thrones and dominion, the Lord of the
Sabbath and the breath of life. In the Garden
of Eden, He is the Tree of life in the midst, and

the Bridegroom whose bride was taken from His bleeding side. In the fall of Adam and Eve, He's the promised Seed of the Woman and the lamb that was sacrificed to cover the shame of our nakedness. In Abel, He's the acceptable sacrifice whose blood speaks forgiveness rather than vengeance. In the genealogy from Adam to Noah, He's the blessed God that came down teaching, whose death brings the despairing rest and comfort. In the flood of Noah, He's the Ark of salvation, Lord of judgement and rainbow of Grace. In Abraham, He's the promised Seed, in whom all the nations of the earth are blessed. In Isaac, He's an obedient Son, a seeker for the bride and the lamb that God Himself provides as sacrifice in our place. In Jacob, He's the ladder connecting Heaven and earth, and in Israel, He's the prince of God. He is a beloved, rejected and exalted son like Joseph, and a son of the right hand like Benjamin.

For by Him all things were created that are in heaven and that are on earth, visible and

**invisible, whether thrones or dominions or
principalities or powers. All things were created
through Him and for Him. And He is before all
things, and in Him all things consist.**
– Colossians 1:16-17

Grace and Truth:

About 2,014 years ago, the God-man Jesus
Christ was born of a young virgin newly-
married to a carpenter, in a lowly stable in the
little town of Bethlehem (the city of David).
The 'Highest High' took on the lowest low by
coming down to earth in human form.
Prophets foretold it (over 300 prophecies
were fulfilled by the first coming of Jesus) and
angels announced it. Lowly shepherds and
learned wise men alike welcomed Him to the
world. Our modern civilization marks His birth
by dividing history into years before Christ
(B.C.) and years after the birth of our Lord:
Anno Domini (A.D.). Jesus Christ was raised
up in Nazareth, a city in the region of Galilee.

At 30 years of age, He was baptised in water by His forerunner: *John the Baptist*, and thereafter anointed without measure by the Holy Spirit. After fasting for 40 days and nights in the Judean wilderness, He was tested vigorously by Satan, and overcame, thereby succeeding where the first man, Adam, failed.

The next day John saw Jesus coming toward him, and said, "Behold! The Lamb of God who takes away the sin of the world!
– John 1:29

In His earthly ministry spanning 3½ years, He healed the sick, deaf, blind and deformed. He cleansed lepers, cast out demons and raised the dead. He fed thousands supernaturally, calmed storms and walked on the sea. He taught as one having authority, showed compassion to sinners, forgave sins and saw into the very heart of men. *Jesus was simply outstanding for no man ever did these things.* He lifted no sword and fought no wars. He had no wife and no children. He had no house to call his own. He sought not to conquer kingdoms, but rather the hearts of men with His love. He committed no sin and no impure thought was ever found in Him. He came to fulfil the Law and the prophets. He taught the best theological sermon ever, teaching men to be humble, meek, merciful, pure in heart, and peacemakers. He also taught us to go the extra mile and to love our enemies. He did not come to condemn but to seek and save the lost. He came to show us the Way!

For the law was given through Moses, but grace and truth came through Jesus Christ.
No one has seen God at any time. The only begotten Son, who is in the bosom of the Father, He has declared Him.
– John 1:16-18

He is the embodiment of grace and truth. Jesus Christ is simply the most outstanding personality that ever lived on this earth. His life, death and resurrection ushered in a new era (covenant), at the onset of the 5th day of man's history (i.e. the first 4 historical days is about 4,000 years from Adam). Just as God prepared the earth for natural life in the first 4 days of creation, even so, mankind was prepared for spiritual life in first 4,000 years of man's history. Therefore, 4 is the number of preparation while 5 is the number of life and grace.

> *Jesus Christ is simply the most outstanding personality that ever lived on this earth.*

He said of Himself: 'Before Abraham was, I AM', 'I am the Way, the Truth and the Life. No one comes to the Father except through Me', 'I am the good shepherd who gives His life for the sheep', 'I am the door. If anyone enters by Me, he will be saved', 'I am the bread of life', 'I and the Father are one', 'I have the power to lay down My life and I have the power to take it again', 'I am the Resurrection and the Life', 'I am the living bread which came down from Heaven' and 'I am the light of the world'.

What is Grace? Grace is God's free gift of *Life Infinite* to mankind. Grace is a person: Jesus Christ. *What is Truth*? Facts may change but Truth is absolute and unchanging. Truth is the Word of God. Truth is a person: Jesus Christ of Nazareth. The power of 'Grace and Truth' is what has been transforming lives across all nations and amongst all peoples over the last 1,985 years. Jesus is still saving lives today!

For God so loved the world that He gave His only begotten Son, that whoever believes in Him should not perish but have everlasting life.
– John 3:16

The Eternal Sacrifice:

Why did *the eternal Word* come down to earth in human flesh? He came to die! He came to pay the penalty for the Sin (rebellion) of Adam and all mankind. He is the pure unblemished supernatural lamb whose blood sacrifice can take away sins. The yearly Jewish Passover is a festival that marks their deliverance from bondage and death over 3,000 years ago. And just as the Passover lamb (unblemished and unspotted) was set apart 4 days before its sacrifice, even so, Jesus Christ was set apart from the very foundations of the world, 4 historical days (i.e. about 4,000 years) before He was crucified on a Passover Friday, about 1,981 years ago.

For the wages of sin is death, but the gift of God is eternal life in Christ Jesus our Lord.
– Romans 6:23

Jesus Christ humbled himself and became obedient, even unto death on the cross. He was wounded, bruised, flogged and scourged. A crown of thorns was driven into His skull. He endured the cross, despising the shame. The pure sinless blood of the Son of God was shed at the cross of Calvary as *the eternal Sacrifice* for Sin. At the cross, He bore the sins of the whole world to the point that He felt forsaken by the Father. It wasn't the nails that kept Him to the cross for He could have walked away at any time. It was His love (compassion) for you and me. He said 'Father forgive them for they know not what they do'. With His last breath, He said 'It is finished', thereby signifying that He had accomplished His mission as *the lamb that was slain*. When the Roman soldiers who crucified Him pierced His side, redemption blood and water gushed out.

For as by one man's disobedience many were made sinners, so also by one Man's obedience many will be made righteous.
– Romans 5:19

At His death, the earth quaked and the sun shut down supernaturally for about 3 hours (from 12noon until 3pm in Jerusalem). The veil in the Jewish temple became torn into two from top to bottom, thereby signifying a new access for all men into the *Holy of Holies*, through the shed blood of Jesus. He died to save us from Sin! The substitutionary death of Jesus Christ as a Passover lamb on the cross is the eternal sacrifice for Sin and the platform for the eternal Salvation of all men. Adam failed the supreme test of obedience at the *tree of good and evil*, and all men became sinners by inheritance. Jesus Christ passed the supreme test of obedience at the *tree (cross) of Calvary (Golgotha)*, so that all men can be made righteous by whole-hearted believing.

For there is one God and one Mediator between God and men, the Man Christ Jesus
– 1 Timothy 2:5

Raised and Seated:

The Cross is Satan's defeat, for at the cross, the *Seed of the Woman* crushed the *head of the serpent* through His pure eternal sacrifice. The devil and his cohorts instigated both Jews and Gentiles to crucify Jesus. Satan thought he had finally got rid of the promised Seed and that Jesus Christ would remain under his prison in hell forever, for Jesus died as a man carrying the sins of other men. However, in

Satan's delusion, he did not perceive that the shed blood of Jesus Christ is the eternal sacrifice that settles the debt of Sin and the punishment of Hell. Satan did not perceive that the justice of the Most High was now served through the cross, and that *the Heavenly Father* was able to raise the man *Jesus Christ* from death and hell through the power of His *Holy Spirit*.

But we speak the wisdom of God in a mystery, the hidden wisdom which God ordained before the ages for our glory, which none of the rulers of this age knew; for had they known, they would not have crucified the Lord of glory.
– 1 Corinthians 2:7-8

On the third day (Easter Sunday), Jesus Christ was resurrected by the Heavenly Father, as the firstborn from the dead, with a new celestial body. He conquered Sin, darkness (spiritual death) and physical death. The resurrection of Jesus Christ is an historical fact which will easily sail through any trial and jury

in our modern legal systems. His tomb was
found empty despite having been heavily
guarded by Roman soldiers. He was seen by
over 500 witnesses over the next 40 days in
different places within Israel, after which He
literally ascended into the highest Heaven in
the presence of some of these witnesses at
the mount called Olivet. Jesus Christ is now
seated at the right hand of the Father in
Heaven, until all His enemies are put under.

**Having disarmed principalities and powers, He
made a public spectacle of them, triumphing over
them in it.**
– Colossians 2:15

Many of the witnesses who saw the
resurrected Jesus touched Him and saw/felt
the crucifixion holes in His hands, feet and
pierced side. Many of the disciples of Jesus
were sore afraid after His crucifixion and hid
themselves. However, after His resurrection,
ascension and their baptism in the Holy Spirit,
these same disciples became bold. Therefore,

from a team of 120 ordinary people grew a Christian church that reached the very ends of the world despite intense persecution from the Jewish leaders and the Roman Empire of that day. Many of these disciples were willing to die for their faith in the resurrected Jesus.

… according to the working of His mighty power which He worked in Christ when He raised Him from the dead and seated Him at His right hand in the heavenly places, far above all principality and power and might and dominion, and every name that is named, not only in this age but also in that which is to come.
– Ephesians 1:19-21

The eternal Word came down from Heaven to do the will of the Father. He left his Heavenly glory and put on the weakness of humanity. He ate as a man, felt tired as a man, slept as a man, worked hard as a man and was tempted as man. He was able to accomplish His mission by embracing an attitude of *Humility* and *Obedience*. The eternal Word honoured the Father while on earth. Therefore, the Father also honoured the Son by making Him Lord of all creation and giving Him a Name that is above every name in all of existence: that wonderful and powerful Name of Jesus.

And being found in appearance as a man, He humbled Himself and became obedient to the point of death, even the death of the cross. Therefore God also has highly exalted Him and given Him the name which is above every name, that at the name of Jesus every knee should bow, of those in heaven, and of those on earth, and of those under the earth, and that every tongue should confess that Jesus Christ is Lord, to the glory of God the Father. – Philippians 2:8-11

The New Birth:

Good works cannot save any man, because no matter how good you are, you are still guilty of Sin and subject to the judgement of a just God. This is why you need a Saviour, someone who can take your place before God. And no other person qualifies as Saviour than the pure unblemished Lamb of God that was slain at the cross of Calvary. When you believe that Jesus Christ is the Son of God, receive Him into your heart as the eternal sacrifice for your sins, and confess with your mouth that Jesus is your Lord, a supernatural event takes place. You become born-again, for *Life Infinite* (eternal life) comes into your darkened spirit (heart), thereby recreating it and restoring you into union and communion with God.

Therefore, if anyone is in Christ, he is a new creation; old things have passed away; behold, all things have become new.
– 2 Corinthians 5:17

When you repent of your sins and trust in Christ Jesus as your Saviour and Lord, you instantly experience a *spiritual* birth into the kingdom of God. You're instantly delivered from the dominion of Satan and translated into the kingdom of Jesus Christ, which is full of *Life, Light and Love*. When you repent and receive the free gift of God, the blood of Jesus cleanses you from all unrighteousness and the Most High comes to dwell within you through His Holy Spirit. Notice that it is your spirit that gets born-again, for God gives you *a new heart* when you believe and receive Jesus. Your soul is progressively renewed and sanctified as you continue daily in studying the Word of God and prayer. Your body will be glorified at the resurrection (Rapture) of the saints. However, for now, you are to put your body under the control of your recreated spirit and present it as holy unto the Lord.

But as many as received Him, to them He gave the right to become children of God, to those who believe in His name. – John 1:12

Benefits of Redemption:

The mathematical formula for victorious living is called: *Substitution*. This is *accessed through faith*. The eternal sacrifice of Jesus Christ is the platform for redemption and the basis for supernatural victory in all circumstances. This is because the sacrifice of Jesus restores the believing man into a legal union with God, such that the dominion lost in Adam is now regained in Christ. This is redemption at work!

The eternal sacrifice of Jesus Christ involves a *seven-fold divine exchange* as follows:

He was punished
that we might be forgiven.
He was wounded
that we might be healed.
He died our death
that we might share His Life.
He endured the curse
that we might enjoy the blessing.
He endured our poverty
that we might share His abundance.
He endured our shame
that we might share His glory.
He endured our rejection
that we might share His acceptance.

For He made Him who knew no sin to be sin for us, that we might become the righteousness of God in Him. – 2 Corinthians 5:21

Jesus Christ became Sin for us, so that we can become Righteousness. We access this by faith when we accept Him as *Saviour*, believe that we are forgiven and cleansed by His blood, and proclaim that we are saved.

that it might be fulfilled which was spoken by Isaiah the prophet, saying: "He Himself took our infirmities And bore our sicknesses."
– Matthew 8:17

Jesus Christ became Sickness for us, so that we can become Health. We access this by faith when we accept Him as *Healer*, believe that we have been healed by His wounds, and proclaim that we are healed and healthy.

For you know the grace of our Lord Jesus Christ, that though He was rich, yet for your sakes He became poor, that you through His poverty might become rich. – 2 Corinthians 8:9

Jesus Christ became Poverty for us, so that we can become abundantly supplied. We access this by faith when we accept Him as *Provider*, believe that we have been delivered from lack and poverty by His sufferings, give tithes and generous offerings in financial partnership with Him, and proclaim that we are abundantly supplied according to God's riches in glory by Christ Jesus. (Phil. 4:19).

Christ has redeemed us from the curse of the law, having become a curse for us (for it is written, "Cursed is everyone who hangs on a tree"), that the blessing of Abraham might come upon the Gentiles in Christ Jesus, that we might receive the promise of the Spirit through faith.
– Galatians 3:13-14

Jesus Christ became Curse for us, so that we can become Blessing. We access this by faith when we accept Him as our *Blessing*, believe that we have been delivered from the curse by His hanging on the tree, and proclaim that we are blessed and a blessing to our world.

Reigning in Life:

The incarnation of the *eternal Word* as Jesus Christ is the first of many. He is the *second man* and the *last Adam* who is called to bring many sons unto glory. Those who believe and receive the eternal sacrifice of Jesus also experience this incarnation, for God comes to dwell inside their hearts (spirits) through His Holy Spirit. Can anything be more powerful than this? *The Greater One* now lives within you. If this is so, why are you still so weak and defeated? Is it because you don't recognise it, believe it, identify with it and proclaim it?

> **… For you are the temple of the living God. As God has said: "I will dwell in them And walk among them. I will be their God, And they shall be My people."**
> −2 Corinthians 6:16

God's will cannot be done on the earth without the cooperation of man. The fact that you're born-again, a child of God, does not leave all the responsibility to God. God will do His part but you have to do yours. Your part is not the supernatural; it's always a natural thing that you can do in obedience to the Word of God. As a follower of Christ, all the promises of God in the Bible belong to you. You now have access by faith to the fullness of GRACE, which can be said to mean: 'God's Riches At Christ's Expense'. It's now your duty to believe the Word and appropriate it in your life on a daily basis. The Word works if you go through the process!

Therefore, having been justified by faith, we have peace with God through our Lord Jesus Christ, through whom also we have access by faith into this grace in which we stand ...
– Romans 5:1-2

The greatest asset that God has given to every person is free will: the ability to make choices. Your will emanates from your spirit and is enacted in your soul. It is your responsibility to repent of your sins and believe the gospel of Jesus. It is your own responsibility to reign in life. It is not all up to God. It is all up to you!

For if by the one man's offense death reigned through the one, much more those who receive abundance of grace and of the gift of righteousness will reign in life through the One, Jesus Christ. – Romans 5:17

As a true believer in Jesus Christ, you have received abundance of grace through Christ and a right standing with God through Christ (i.e. the same standing of Christ) so that you can reign as a king in your domain in this life through Christ. What are you to reign over? Sin, sickness, disease, poverty, oppression, depression, demons, and every other form of spiritual darkness. You have been raised and seated, together with Christ (Eph. 2:6). *What are you doing with what you have received*?

For whatever is born of God overcomes the world. And this is the victory that has overcome the world—our faith. – 1 John 5:4

Man's Responsibility:

In the natural life, we know that nothing gets done unless someone acts. For example, when you wake up at dawn, you may decide to either go back to sleep or to get up. The choice is yours and so are the consequences. The same principles apply spiritually for we always reap what we sow, with the exception of mercy drops. And why live on mercy drops when you have access by faith to the fullness of grace and truth; the fullness of divine life?

Faith is a spiritual law, just like the natural law of gravity. How faith works is not random and faith is not a wish list. The principles of faith are revealed throughout the Bible. They can be learned and mastered just like any other field of study. The mere fact that you cannot perform a surgery does not mean that surgeons are 'lucky magicians' or that surgery is ineffective. If only you could apply yourself to enthusiastic study and persevering practice under guidance of accomplished surgeons, you will be able to make a success of it one day. The same process works with faith.

So then faith comes by hearing, and hearing by the word of God.
– Romans 10:17

It is your responsibility to study and meditate on the Word of God daily because it feeds your spirit and renews your mind. It is your responsibility to believe the Word of God concerning your situation, to identify with what the Word says that you are in Christ, and to proclaim it over your situation. It is your responsibility to claim your healing, supply, deliverance and victory by faith. It is your responsibility to refuse to be worried about anything, to pray regularly in the Spirit, to give thanks in everything, and to rejoice in the Lord always. It is your responsibility to pay your tithes and give offerings as part of your financial partnership with God. It is your responsibility to take corresponding actions in line with your faith, maintain your ground on the Word, and persevere in your faith. It is your responsibility to resist and rebuke the devil. It is your responsibility to take good care of (and to glorify God in) your body.

The greatest asset that God has given to every person is free will: the ability to make choices.

Note that the devil is a tempter and an attempter. *He will try to put anything on anybody*. Stand your ground on what the Word says about you and don't back off. The devil may roar with adverse circumstances, but you are to stand firm and maintain your ground on the Rock of ages (i.e. the Word of God). When you resist the devil steadfastly, he has to flee from you (1 Pet. 5:8-9).

Therefore submit to God. Resist the devil and he will flee from you. – James 4:7

Many Christians may wonder why they are not winning. Well now, if all you ever gave attention to was secular entertainment, secular refreshment, secular training and secular pursuits, how could you ever achieve anything spiritual or supernatural? You've got to give quality attention to spiritual food (the Word) and to spiritual drink (the Spirit). You've got to give quality attention to faith and obedience, communion with God, walking in love, and fellowship with believers. You have a personal responsibility to believe and appropriate the Word for yourself. If you have faith as small as a mustard seed, you will SAY and SPEAK to your mountain. If you are not speaking your faith, it remains dormant and ineffective, for death and life are in the power of the tongue. What have you been saying?

SAY THIS OUT: I believe in the eternal sacrifice of Jesus Christ. I accept Him as my Lord. I believe in the divine exchange He paid for me. Therefore, I am a child of God and He is my Father. He dwells in me by His Holy Spirit. I have a right standing with Him because of Jesus Christ. His life, light and love are dominating me today. Therefore I reign over Sin, sickness and all darkness. Amen!

For with the heart one believes unto righteousness, and with the mouth confession is made unto salvation.
– Romans 10:10

Hindrances to Winning:

1. Lack of Repentance
Saying sorry to God (and others) when you've done wrong, and meaning it from your heart, releases you from the power of Sin. *Be quick to repent* and confess your sins before God. Do not let sin linger in your heart for one moment, for it hinders your communion with God. *Saying sorry and meaning it is one of the most important things you will do on this side of eternity.* When you confess your wrong-doing to God, He forgives you and cleanses you with the precious blood of Jesus Christ.

If we confess our sins, He is faithful and just to forgive us our sins and to cleanse us from all unrighteousness. – 1 John 1:9

2. Lack of Forgiveness

Just as it is important to repent of your sins, it is equally important to forgive others, including yourself. If we don't forgive others, how can we expect God to forgive us? Unforgiveness is a spiritual poison that hinders the flow of blessing. *Be quick to forgive.* Whenever you're finding it difficult to forgive, think about all that Jesus went through at the cross, for you. You forgive them because of Jesus!

> **"And whenever you stand praying, if you have anything against anyone, forgive him, that your Father in heaven may also forgive you your trespasses. But if you do not forgive, neither will your Father in heaven forgive your trespasses."**
> – Mark 11:25-26

3. Unbelief and Disobedience

Unbelief is the great neutraliser to victorious living. It is characterised by either doubt or fear. Unbelief always leads to disobedience. God is neither emotional nor erratic. He rewards faith and obedience. He cannot bless unbelief and disobedience. The solution to unbelief is giving *attention* to the truth and meditating on it. God's Word is Truth and Truth casts out unbelief. *Be quick to believe* the Word. Choose to trust God rather than circumstances. There is no fear in love!

So Jesus said to them, "Because of your UNBELIEF; for assuredly, I say to you, if you have faith as a mustard seed, YOU WILL SAY to this mountain, 'Move from here to there,' and it will move; and nothing will be impossible for you.
– Matthew 17:20

4. Pride and Prejudice
The greatest limitation in life is 'pride and prejudice'. Pride usually manifests itself as a bloated ego, excessive self-importance, superiority complex, stubbornness, an unteachable attitude and false humility. Its mate, prejudice, will always lead to wrong believing, for it is so biased or self-assured that it is not willing to change opinion even in

the presence of Truth. *God resists the proud but gives grace to the humble* (James 4:6-10).

The greatest limitation in every person's life is their 'pride and prejudice'.

5. Selfishness
Selfishness means wanting your own way and everything for yourself, without appropriate consideration for others. A selfish person is inconsiderate and insensitive. *Selfishness is at the root of every sin.* When you receive Christ, the love of God is shed abroad in your heart by the Holy Spirit. However, it is important to walk in that love and give it expression. Let that love blossom by learning to focus on Jesus. Love is patient and kind. It is generous and large-hearted. Love cares about others and seeks their progress. *What you need in life is God-esteem, rather than self-esteem.*

Love does no harm to a neighbour; therefore love is the fulfilment of the law.
– Romans 13:10

6. A careless Tongue

The tongue is your most powerful body part. It is an instrument of releasing power, whether positive or negative. Abstain from careless and idle talking. Choose your words wisely. Don't negate your prayers with a negative confession. Learn to put the Word of God on your mouth. Say only what you hear your Heavenly Father say. Keep saying the Word of God, even in the midst of opposition and adverse circumstances. Facts do change but Truth remains. *Your confession is Satan's defeat*. A wholesome tongue can be achieved by habitually putting the Word on your mouth and praying in the Spirit. A wholesome tongue is full of praise and thanksgiving.

Death and life are in the power of the tongue, And those who love it will eat its fruit.
– Proverbs 18:21

7. Laziness

Laziness is evading or compromising critical action. It is a cankerworm that destroys divine destinies. It robs men of their potential and God's best for them. Laziness is not spiritual; it is a work of the flesh. *You may be busy but yet lazy.* Laziness usually expresses itself as procrastination or comfortable compromise, i.e. evading the right action and taking the easy way out. God will not honour laziness, for He is a rewarder of them that diligently seek Him. *Laziness will hinder your mission in life.* There is only one solution to laziness: Do the right thing at the right time. Always remember that *His grace is sufficient* for you and that *you can do all things through Christ* who strengthens you.

that you do not become sluggish, but imitate those who through faith and patience inherit the promises. – Hebrews 6:12

Now thanks be to God who always leads us in triumph in Christ, and through us diffuses the fragrance of His knowledge in every place. – 2 Corinthians 2:14

CHAPTER 6
WHERE AM I GOING TO?

The Appointment:

It is universally known that every living person on earth has an appointment with death. Given this unavoidable fact, the important question is: *what happens when we die*? As discussed in Chapter 3, man is a spirit (spiritual realm) who has a soul (intellectual realm) and lives in a body (physical realm). Physical death is therefore the termination of life from the body. However, the spirit and soul continue to live on. Spirits are immortal. They do not go into annihilation but exist forever in either eternal light (eternal life) or eternal darkness (eternal death). We have only one life to live in this natural body, and when a person dies, his *natural life* on this earth is over forever.

And as it is appointed for men to die once, but after this the judgment – Hebrews 9:27

Do not be deceived, for there is no such thing as *reincarnation*. The next question is: *what determines our afterlife?* Life is probation. Your performance (faith and works) in life determines your eternal place and state.

Spirits are immortal. They do not go into annihilation but exist forever in either eternal light or eternal darkness

Your eternal place is determined by your faith. Good works cannot save any man, because no matter how good you are, you are still guilty of Sin and subject to the judgement of a *Just* God. This is why you need a Saviour, someone who can stand in your place before God. And no other person qualifies as Saviour than the pure unblemished Lamb of God that was slain at the cross of Calvary. When you believe in Him and receive Him as your Saviour and Lord, you are saved from Hell (eternal death, eternal darkness) and you become a citizen of Heaven (eternal life, eternal light).

If you reject the Most High and refuse to worship Him in this life, despite the eternal sacrifice of Jesus Christ on your behalf, you would have no excuse at all. All that is left is eternal judgement.

For if we sin willfully after we have received the knowledge of the truth, there no longer remains a sacrifice for sins, but a certain fearful expectation of judgment, and fiery indignation which will devour the adversaries.
– Hebrews 10:26-27

If God were to withdraw the sun and the rain from the earth for one year, that gives us a starting idea of what Hell is. Remember, He made and owns the sun, moon, stars, clouds, sky and seas. Most importantly, He made you and He owns you. That is the very reason why you should live to worship Him: your design-purpose in life. The question is not how a loving God could send anyone to hell. The question is how anyone could reject a loving God. The price of Sin has been fully paid in

Jesus Christ, the Son of God. Now, it's all up to you to repent, receive and follow Him. It's your choice, your move, and your destiny.

He who believes in Him is not condemned; but he who does not believe is condemned already, because he has not believed in the name of the only begotten Son of God.
– John 3:18

Your eternal state is determined by your works. There are different degrees of glory and honour in Heaven. This corresponds to how faithful a believer is, in their obedience to God's Word, for God rewards those that diligently seek Him. In like manner, there are different degrees of suffering and torment in Hell. This corresponds to how rebellious an unbeliever is, in their disobedience to God's Word, for God will repay everyone for how they lived their lives on earth.

And you, Capernaum, who are exalted to heaven, will be brought down to Hades; for if the mighty

works which were done in you had been done in Sodom, it would have remained until this day. But I say to you that it shall be more tolerable for the land of Sodom in the day of judgment than for you. – Matthew 11:23-24

What happens immediately after death? The transition to our eternal place happens the very moment we die. For in the true-life story of the rich (ungodly) man and Lazarus (Luke 16:19-31), we are told by the Lord Jesus that when the rich man died, he was buried and immediately found himself in the torment of *Hades* (Hell). On the other hand, Lazarus died and was carried straight to Abraham's bosom (i.e. Paradise). Furthermore, Jesus assured the 'repentant and believing' thief at the cross that he will join Him in Paradise on the same day, i.e. immediately after their death.

Then he said to Jesus, "Lord, remember me when You come into Your kingdom." And Jesus said to him, "Assuredly, I say to you, today you will be with Me in Paradise."
– Luke 23:42-43

Do not be deceived. There is no partying in hell. There is no fun in Hell. Hell is a literal place, where the goodness of God is totally absent. It is a place full of darkness, sorrow, regret, torment, pain and hopelessness.

Life is probation. Your performance in life determines your eternal status.

The Rapture:

Although every person is appointed to die once, there are some people who will not taste death at all. Rather, they will be raptured (caught up and literally translated) into the highest Heaven by the power of the Most High. This phenomenon has previously occurred with two men in history: Enoch, the 7th from Adam, and Elijah the prophet. Jesus Christ also ascended (was raptured) into Heaven after His resurrection from the dead. He is the firstborn from the dead, for God raised him up with a new celestial (immortal) body. Furthermore, He is the head of the true church (His body), which also is the bride taken from His pierced and bleeding side. And just as Christ the head of the church was raptured into Heaven about 1,981 years ago, even so must His body, the true church (consisting of both living and dead saints), be raptured to join Him, so that bridegroom and bride can be together for their wedding ceremony in Heaven. Jesus promised His disciples that just as He would be literally raptured from them, even so was He going to come back to receive them to Himself, so that they can be together forever.

In My Father's house are many mansions; if it were not so, I would have told you. I go to prepare a place for you. And if I go and prepare a place for you, I will come again and receive you to Myself; that where I am, there you may be also. – John 14:2-3

The rapture is an exciting event. This is because all living believers (abiding in Christ) at this time will not taste death. Rather, they will be instantly caught up and their bodies changed from mortal to immortal. Genuine Christians from all over the world would disappear from the earth in the twinkling of an eye. They will join all the resurrected saints from the church age, to meet the Lord in the air. The rapture is the end of the church age!

For the Lord Himself will descend from heaven with a shout, with the voice of an archangel, and with the trumpet of God. And the dead in Christ will rise first. Then we who are alive and remain shall be caught up together with them in the clouds to meet the Lord in the air. And thus we shall always be with the Lord.
– 1 Thessalonians 4:16-17

It is important to note that the Rapture is an imminent event. Just as the betrothed bride (in Bible times) is kept in *suspense* about when her bridegroom will arrive to take her for the wedding ceremony, even so is the arrival of Jesus Christ for His bride: the true church. No man knows the day nor the hour (Matt. 24:36-44). The only way to prepare for the Rapture is to be always ready, by continuing in the faith and living a life that is well-pleasing to the Lord. The rapture is the *Blessed Hope* of true believers in Christ. It is definitely something to look forward to, as this will energise your walk with God. The rapture of true believers in Christ is approaching fast. Don't be left behind!

looking for the blessed hope and glorious appearing of our great God and Savior Jesus Christ – Titus 2:13

The Judgement Seat:

The true church which has been raptured from the earth will pass through the judgement seat of Christ, for *purification* and *reward*. Although true believers in Christ are saved by grace through faith, they will still have to give account for how they lived their lives while on earth and how faithfully they obeyed their Lord and master, Jesus Christ. This is why the Bible encourages believers in Christ to be fervent in spirit, serving the Lord.

Therefore we make it our aim, whether present or absent, to be well pleasing to Him. For we must all appear before the judgment seat of Christ, that each one may receive the things done in the body, according to what he has done, whether good or bad.
– 2 Corinthians 5:9-10

Life is probation. Whatever we sow in this life is what we reap thereafter. Our lifetime on earth is a time of worship and service to the Lord. *Laziness is not spiritual and lazy believers will lose their rewards.* Anything we do in this life that does not *ultimately contribute* to the purpose of God (*worship*) and the plan of God (*redemption*) is a waste of time. Whatever your daily occupation is, you can use it to honour and glorify God. Paying your tithes regularly and training up your children in the way of the Lord is a starter.

For no other foundation can anyone lay than that which is laid, which is Jesus Christ. Now if anyone builds on this foundation with gold, silver, precious stones, wood, hay, straw, each one's work will become clear; for the Day will declare it, because it will be revealed by fire; and the fire will test each one's work, of what sort it is. If anyone's work which he has built on it endures, he will receive a reward. If anyone's work is burned, he will suffer loss; but he himself will be saved, yet so as through fire.
– 1 Corinthians 3:11-15

Will you appear before your Lord and master empty-handed, with nothing to show for your lifetime on the earth? Start living for Him! The works that will survive the judgement seat are those that are done in *faith and obedience* to the Lord. All bad works (selfish motives and false doctrines) will be consumed by fire, for Christ must present the church to Himself as a glorious church. Don't lose your rewards! Don't lose your crowns! Start building your eternal inheritance with good quality material: *faith, hope and love* (1 Cor. 13:13).

**that He might sanctify and cleanse her with the
washing of water by the word, that He might
present her to Himself a glorious church, not
having spot or wrinkle or any such thing, but that
she should be holy and without blemish.**
– Ephesians 5:26-27

The Tribulation:

The tribulation is a 7-year period of
unparalleled turmoil on the whole earth, for
at this time the judgements of God are
poured on a rebellious world and the man of
Sin, the antichrist, is allowed to reign over the
nations of the earth. The tribulation is
triggered by the rapture of the saints, for the
Spirit-filled church is the restraining factor on
the full explosion of evil in our world today.
The Day of the Lord (*Rapture–Tribulation–
Armageddon–Millennium*) so comes (begins)
as a thief in the night (1 Thess. 5:1-10). Those
who are *left behind* after the rapture of the
saints are unbelievers and false believers (the

apostate church, which is also the church of the Laodiceans that consists of lukewarm unbelievers as explained in Rev. 3:14-22).

For the mystery of lawlessness is already at work; only He who now restrains will do so until He is taken out of the way. And then the lawless one will be revealed, whom the Lord will consume with the breath of His mouth and destroy with the brightness of His coming.
– 2 Thessalonians 2:7-8

The man called antichrist is the 'son of perdition'. Those who reject the 'grace and truth' of Jesus Christ will suffer an endurance of the wrath of God under the antichrist: that Satanic man of sin (the beast) who will reign over the world in the tribulation period: the last 7 years of man's rule on the earth. The second half of the tribulation is called the *Great Tribulation*. Those who have hardened their hearts against the Most High will be deceived into worshipping the antichrist and pledging eternal allegiance to him by taking the *mark of the beast* on their right hands or on their foreheads. No one will be allowed to buy or sell without the mark. Those who worship the beast and receive his mark will be *eternally damned*, for the worship of *the antichrist* is the ultimate form of rebellion against God. The number of the name of the beast (antichrist) is the number of a man: 666 (2 Thess. 2:9-12, Rev. 13:16-18). The antichrist and his cohorts will also be used to judge and destroy the false 'apostate' church (the great harlot which had connived with him to persecute the saints) at this time.

... "If anyone worships the beast and his image, and receives his mark on his forehead or on his hand, he himself shall also drink of the wine of the wrath of God ... He shall be tormented with fire and brimstone ... And the smoke of their torment ascends forever and ever; and they have no rest day or night, who worship the beast and his image, and whoever receives the mark of his name." – Revelation 14:9-11

However, for many of those who are *left behind* after the rapture, all hope is not lost. This is because the tribulation period is also an extension of God's mercy to bring the sinner to repentance. *The eternal sacrifice of Jesus Christ will always be valid for Salvation of the living*. If you find yourself in the tribulation, all you need do is to repent of Sin, believe in Jesus Christ and receive Him into your life as Saviour and Lord. By so doing, you will become part of *the tribulation saints*, for God will continue to redeem the souls of repentant men during the tribulation period. *Do not worship the beast, do not pledge allegiance to him and do not receive his mark*! You may probably have to lose your life for believing in Christ and refusing to worship the antichrist but your eternal salvation is well worth the sacrifice.

It was granted to him to make war with the saints and to overcome them. And authority was given him over every tribe, tongue, and nation. All who dwell on the earth will worship him,

whose names have not been written in the Book of Life of the Lamb slain from the foundation of the world. – Revelation 13:7-8

The Return of the King:

At the end of the great tribulation period, the Lord Jesus Christ will return physically to the earth with His newly-wedded bride (i.e. resurrected saints from the church age). Every eye will see Him coming with the clouds. The antichrist, the kings of the earth and their armies will gather to fight the Lord Jesus Christ and His saints in the battle of *Armageddon* but they all will be defeated and destroyed. All those who reject Christ will be destroyed at this time. The antichrist and his false prophet will be cast into the *lake of fire and brimstone*, as the very first occupants of that *eternal monument of the rebellious* which was initially reserved for the devil and his fallen angels (Rev. 19:11-21).

Behold, He is coming with clouds, and every eye will see Him, even they who pierced Him. And all the tribes of the earth will mourn because of Him. Even so, Amen.
– Revelation 1:7

The *millennium* is the 1,000-year peaceful reign of the Lord Jesus Christ on the earth. It is the fullness of the Day of the Lord, the age to come, the Sabbath of the Lord, the earth's rest and the restoration of all things. During this time, Satan will be bound in the *Abyss* (*bottomless pit*), so that he should deceive the nations no more. The *millennium* will begin with the marriage supper (feast) of *the Lamb* (i.e. wedding reception) and this will include the bridegroom (Jesus Christ), His bride (the raptured church), friends of the bridegroom (saints before the church age and tribulation martyrs, all now resurrected) and friends of the bride (tribulation saints alive at that time).

Then he said to me, "Write: 'Blessed are those who are called to the marriage supper of the

Lamb!'" And he said to me, "These are the true sayings of God." – Revelation 19:9

The *millennium* is the Sabbath day of history which will be ruled over by the Lord of the Sabbath: Jesus Christ. He will bring rest, healing and restoration to the earth.

The wolf and the lamb shall feed together,
The lion shall eat straw like the ox,
And dust shall be the serpent's food.
They shall not hurt nor destroy in all My holy mountain," Says the LORD – Isaiah 65:25

The Great White Throne:

After the 1,000-year millennial reign of Christ, during which a new generation would have arisen from the tribulation saints alive at the start of the millennium, Satan will be released from the *Abyss* (bottomless pit) in order to have one final turn at deceiving the nations. Those born during the millennium, having seen and experienced the direct glory of the Lord Jesus Christ on earth, will still have to face the ultimate test of *faith and obedience*.

Life is probation. Your performance in life determines your eternal status.

It is amazing to find that many will still be deceived to join forces with Satan to make war with the King of kings and Lord of lords. They will all be devoured by fire from Heaven. And finally, having completed *a mission of failure and shame* in his rebellion against God, the devil (Satan) will be cast into the lake *of fire and brimstone* to join the antichrist and the false prophet. They will be tormented day and night forever and ever in that *eternal monument of the rebellious* (Rev. 20:7-10).

Then I saw a great white throne and Him who sat on it, from whose face the earth and the heaven fled away. And there was found no place for them. And I saw the dead, small and great, standing before God, and BOOKS WERE OPENED.

And another book was opened, which is the Book of Life. And the dead were judged according to their WORKS, by the things which were written in the BOOKS. – Revelation 20:11-12

After the final sentencing of Satan and his cohorts, all the dead unbelievers from all generations of men over the 7,000 years of man's history will be resurrected to face *the great white throne of the Most High*. All will be judged according to their works. The purpose of this judgement is for final sentencing, for their eternal destiny was already sealed from the moment they died without *faith in the Most High (Jesus Christ)*.

Good works cannot save you, only faith in Jesus.

The good works of unbelievers cannot save them for they are still guilty of Sin, the greatest of which is the rejection of the Most High (Jesus Christ) as their personal Lord and King. Their sentence will be according to how rebellious they lived while on earth. There are different degrees of suffering and torment in Hell. This corresponds to how rebellious an unbeliever is, in their disobedience to God's Word, for God will repay everyone for how they lived their lives on earth.

The sea gave up the dead who were in it, and Death and Hades delivered up the dead who were in them. And they were judged, each one according to his works. Then Death and Hades were cast into the lake of fire. This is the second death. And anyone not found written in THE BOOK OF LIFE was cast into the lake of fire.
– Revelation 20:13-15

It is only a whole-hearted acceptance of *the eternal sacrifice* of Jesus Christ on the cross of Calvary that keeps your name in *the book of life*. Anyone not found written in the book of life will be cast into the *lake of fire and brimstone*. They will be tormented day and night forever and ever in that *eternal monument of the rebellious* (Rev. 20:7-10). If we reject Jesus Christ in this life, He will reject us for ALL eternity. If we accept Jesus Christ in this life, He will accept us for ALL eternity. The choice is yours to make NOW. Don't delay for tomorrow may be too late. Eternal Heaven glorifies God and His justice. Eternal Hell also glorifies God and His justice. In all of eternity, God must be glorified.

Unquenchable fire (eternal death) is the final judgement for rebellion against the Most High

Eternity:

After the sentencing of all unbelievers to the eternal lake of fire and brimstone, the current heavens and earth will pass away. They will be replaced by a new heaven and a new earth. The holy city of the Most High, the *New Jerusalem*, will come down from Heaven to earth, full of infinite glory. God will come to dwell with His people forever and ever. The city is made of pure gold, like clear glass. Its walls are made of 12 precious stones: jasper, sapphire, chalcedony, emerald, sardonyx, sardius, chrysolite, beryl, topaz, chrysoprase, jacinth, and amethyst (Rev. 21:1-27). A modern study of these stones shows exclusive matching properties for building and lighting.

The city had no need of the sun or of the moon to shine in it, for the glory of God illuminated it. The Lamb is its light. And the nations of those who are saved shall walk in its light, and the kings of the earth bring their glory and honor into it.
– Revelation 21:22-24

Eternity is the 8th day of man's history, when time will be no more. It is characterised by all things being made new. Therefore, 8 is the number of new beginnings, and also the number of infinity. Furthermore, 888 is the number of the name of *Jesus*, which signifies the new covenant of God with men.

Then He who sat on the throne said, Behold, I make all things new." And He said to me, "Write, for these words are true and faithful."
– Revelation 21:5

He who overcomes shall inherit all things, and I will be his God and he shall be My son. But the cowardly, unbelieving, abominable, murderers, sexually immoral, sorcerers, idolaters, and all liars shall have their part in the lake which burns with fire and brimstone, which is the second death – Revelation 21:7-8

Wisdom:

It is important to note that the Most High is also a mathematician, since He is the source of all knowledge and wisdom. Let us consider the following Biblical truths:

3 is the number of divine completeness
4 is the number of preparation
5 is the number of life and grace
6 is the number of man
7 is the number of spiritual perfection
7 is the number of rest and Sabbath
8 is the number of new beginnings
1 day (with the Lord) = 1000 years (with man)

666 is the number of the name of antichrist
888 is the number of the name of Jesus

Using these truths, we can make some deductions about the history of man and the end of time.

1. The earthly ministry of Jesus will be *completed* within 3 historical days = 3000 years. This refers to the 5th, 6th and 7th day of history, for Jesus was incarnated towards the end of the 4th historical day of *preparation*.

2. The 7th day of history is a day of *rest*, the *Sabbath* of the Lord, which corresponds to the 1,000 year millennial reign of Jesus Christ on the earth, for He is Lord of the *Sabbath*.

3. Man's rule over the earth will be completed in the 6th day of history, which corresponds to end of the 2nd historical day (i.e. 2,000 years) from the cross of Christ. Man's rule will be completed with the reign of *the man* of sin, also called the antichrist.

4. Just as Christ the head was resurrected at the onset of the 3rd day, and within 2 days, from the cross, even so must the true church, body of Christ, be resurrected at the onset of the 3rd historical day, and within 2 historical days = 2,000 years, from the beginning of Christ's earthly ministry.

5. We are fast approaching the end of the 6th day of history which completes the years given to man's rule. This also corresponds to the end of the 2nd historical day from Christ (i.e. 2,000 years from the death of Christ in AD33).

These simple mathematical deductions from the Bible show us that *we are the last generation*. Most of those reading this book will witness the *Rapture*. Many will witness the *Great Tribulation* and the tyrannical reign of antichrist. It is my prayer that you will be *saved from wrath by trusting in Jesus*.

For this is good and acceptable in the sight of God our Savior, who desires all men to be saved and to come to the knowledge of the truth.
– 1 Timothy 2:3-4

It is my prayer that you will remain in Christ and be raptured ('caught up') to meet Him in the air, thereby escaping the *tribulation*. It is my prayer that you will partake of the peaceful restorative millennial reign of Jesus Christ on the earth. It is my prayer that you will reign with Jesus Christ forever in the new heavens and the new earth to come. Beware of the religious spirit which has to do with forms, traditions and ceremonies. God is seeking for *true worshippers* (John 4:23-24): those who will worship Him in spirit (with all their heart) and in truth (without hypocrisy).

And he said to me, "Do not seal the words of the prophecy of this book, for the time is at hand. He who is unjust, let him be unjust still; he who is filthy, let him be filthy still; he who is righteous, let him be righteous still; he who is holy, let him be holy still." – Revelation 22:10-11

Choice:

What will you do with Jesus Christ, the Son of God? This is the ultimate question that determines your eternal destiny. If you believe, receive and follow Him, you have chosen *excellently*. If you reject Him and turn back from Him, you have chosen *very poorly*. The choice is yours *now* but not forever. Now is the accepted time. Now is the day of salvation. Beware of pride and prejudice!

"And behold, I am coming quickly, and My reward is with Me, to give to every one according to his work. I am the Alpha and the Omega, the Beginning and the End, the First and the Last."
– Revelation 22:12-13

CHAPTER 7
WHAT TO DO NOW?

Walk with God:

Your walk with God is your personal act of worship. A Christian is a disciple (committed follower) of Christ, and not just a fan. The keywords for walking with God are *faith and obedience*. It is by faith that Enoch walked with God to the point that he was raptured and did not taste death. Live by faith and walk by faith, for it is only faith that pleases God (Heb. 11:5-6, Gen. 5:21-24). Faith without corresponding actions is dead. *There is no faith without obedience.* Jesus said that His sheep hear His voice and that those who really love Him keep His commandments.

As you therefore have received Christ Jesus the Lord, so WALK in Him, rooted and built up in Him and established in the faith, as you have been taught, abounding in it with thanksgiving.
– Colossians 2:6-7

Walking with God involves you *spending time* in *personal* communion and fellowship with Him. Remember that *God is relational* and He made you for personal relationship with Him.

Imagine what it will be like to go through a day without food and drink or to go through months without proper food and drink. Many Christians are spiritually starving, constipated, or dehydrated. And this is because they are not eating spiritual food daily and drinking spiritual drink daily. If you spend all your time (whether deliberately or carelessly) doing worldly things, you will remain a *spiritual baby* or *spiritual child*, irrespective of how many years that you have been a Christian.

Carelessness is not an excuse. We make time for things that are really important to us.

If all you ever gave attention to was secular entertainment, secular refreshment, secular training and secular pursuits, how could you ever achieve anything spiritual? You,ve got to *give quality attention* to spiritual food (the Word) and to spiritual drink (the Spirit).

My son, give ATTENTION to my words;
INCLINE your ear to my sayings.
Do not let them depart from your eyes;
Keep them in the midst of your heart;
For they are LIFE to those who FIND them,
And HEALTH to all their FLESH.
KEEP your heart with all DILIGENCE,
For out of it SPRING the issues of life.
– Proverbs 4:20-23

In this last generation where iniquity abounds, many Christians are allowing technology to destroy their walk with God. *Christians have become addicted to entertainment rather than being addicted to the Word.* Technology is a dummy, and you can take the initiative over its use. Deliberately decide what content you want to be exposed to. *A little leaven is all that it takes to leaven the whole lump* (Luke 13:20-21, 1 Cor. 5:6-7). The secular media is not committed to your spiritual growth. On the contrary, they are committed to eroding your walk with God. Don't spend all your time downloading language, violence and nudity (obscenities, profanities, cursing, flirting, seduction, immorality, murder, assault, horror, drunkenness and perversion) into your precious soul (Phil. 4:8). Rather, make use of technology to enhance your study of the Word of God (online, tablet, smartphone, TV, and audio/video player) everywhere you find yourself. The opportunities are near limitless!

Technology is a dummy. Exploit it for your spiritual growth. Study the Word of God using every technology available.

Is Jesus Christ your Lord? If so, start living for Him! Make Him the very centre of your life. Let His Word have your full attention. Make out time for prayer and meditation daily. Praise Him abundantly! Live victoriously in life by focussing on Jesus. Don't mess about with sin and appearances of evil. Learn to say sorry (either to the Lord or to your fellow men) when you're wrong, and do it as often as the situation arises, for this has the power to keep your heart and conscience tender before God. Walk in sacrificial love (the God-kind) and maintain a humble attitude. Always put the Word of God on your mouth. Say only what you hear your Heavenly Father say. Develop a working relationship with the Holy Spirit, and pray in the Spirit at all times. Live out *Zoe* (divine life) to the full and become all that God has designed you to be in Christ.

Let your garments always be white,
And let your head lack no oil.
– Ecclesiastes 9:8

VICTORY CONFESSION:
My Bible is the written Word of God.
The Word of God is true, alive and powerful.
I study and meditate on the Word. I believe the
Word. I confess the Word. I live by the Word.
I am what the Word says I am.
I can do what the Word says I can do.
The anointed Word will set me free.
Glory to God! Hallelujah! Amen!

Fellowship with Believers:

Your fellowship with other believers is your cooperate act of worship. The church is the body of Christ and if you are a Christian, you belong to this body. The church is not man's idea; it was instituted by Jesus Christ Himself. He prayed that all true believers may be perfectly united, in same manner as the Father, Son and Holy Spirit (John 17:1-26). Always remember that your Christian walk cannot be complete until you unite with other true believers in a local church.

> **"I do not pray for these alone, but also for those who will believe in Me through their word; that they ALL MAY BE ONE, as You, Father, are in Me, and I in You; that they also may be one in Us, that the world may believe that You sent Me.**
> — John 17:20-21

Make sure to join a *living* church where the 'Word and Spirit' are given utmost importance, the selfless overflowing love of

God is practised, and a faith walk in Christ is actively encouraged. Your consistency in attending church meetings has a great impact on your spiritual growth (Heb. 10:23-25).

And let us consider one another in order to stir up love and good works, NOT FORSAKING THE ASSEMBLING of ourselves together, as is the manner of some, but exhorting one another, and so much the more as you see the Day approaching. – Hebrews 10:24-25

It is not enough to attend church only for *worship service* on Sundays (i.e. on the Lord's day). True Christianity is a lifestyle that is integrated with all you are and everything you do. Other church meetings such as *home group, bible study, prayer meeting, outreach and socials* are also very important because they contribute significantly to your spiritual growth. It is God's perfect will that you grow to become like Christ and to do that, you need the *encouragement* of other believers. You need the church and the church needs you!

And He Himself gave some to be apostles, some prophets, some evangelists, and some PASTORS AND TEACHERS, for the EQUIPPING of the saints for the WORK of ministry, for the EDIFYING of the BODY of Christ, till we all come to the UNITY of the faith and of the knowledge of the Son of God, to a PERFECT man, to the measure of the stature of the FULLNESS OF CHRIST;
– Ephesians 4:11-13

Serve The Lord:

Your service to the Lord is your functional act of worship. Jesus Christ is the Son of God, yet He came 'down to earth' to serve and save others. In the same manner, all Christians are sons and also servants of God. Your service to the lord is not like you're doing Him a favour. You have been called from day one to serve Him, for He is now your Lord and master (John 13:12-16). The purpose of Christian service is to fulfil the eternal plan of God: *Redemption*. Christ the head can only *function* through His body on the earth. You are a very important part of this body and your service is *essential*.

just as the Son of Man did not come to be served, but TO SERVE, and to give His life a ransom for many." – Matthew 20:28

The basic principle of all Christian service is giving, for freely we have received of His grace and freely we must give (John 1:16, Matt. 10:8). Our service to the Lord involves giving freely (and sacrificially) of our money, time, talents, resources and capabilities. Giving is an act of *faith and obedience*. We give because we trust God and we belong to Him. Our faith pleases God and He rewards obedience. Giving is a spiritual principle which leads to increase. God loves a cheerful giver!

Give, and it will be given to you: good measure, pressed down, shaken together, and running over will be put into your bosom. For with the same measure that you use, it will be measured back to you." – Luke 6:38

The foundational step to your Christian service is paying your tithes (i.e. 10% of your income) to your local church. Are you in financial partnership with God? Are you worshipping God with your money? What percentage of your income do you think that God's work deserves? Giving generously is not about numbers. It is about percentages. Tithing is the starting point (training wheels) of generous giving. (Mal. 3:10, 2 Cor. 9:8). Your tithe is not optional; it is an act of obedience and gratitude, with expectation of blessing.

> **"No one can serve two masters; for either he will hate the one and love the other, or else he will be loyal to the one and despise the other. You cannot serve God and mammon** (money)**.**
> – Matthew 6:24

Christians need to understand that the devil is very keen to hinder the work of God on the earth, and a major way to do this is by getting them to withhold their tithes, for this deprives the local church of a regular income for doing the Lord's work. Why should you spend more money on 'restaurants and tips' than you give to your Lord? Why should you spend more money on 'clothes and toys' than you give to your Lord? Why should you spend more money on 'entertainment' than you give to your Lord? Actually, we haven't really given until we've paid our tithes. Tithing is not the last word in generosity; it's the first word. You should pay your tithe where you receive spiritual nourishment (e.g. your local church). You should give offerings over and above your tithes. You should give alms or donations to poor and charity. You should pay your tithe as a first fruit, as soon as you receive *any income*, lest you're tempted to spend it.

But this I say: He who sows sparingly will also reap sparingly, and he who sows bountifully will also reap bountifully ... Now may He who supplies SEED TO THE SOWER, and bread for food, supply and multiply the seed you have sown and increase the fruits of your righteousness – 2 Corinthians 9:6-10

The Lord supplies *seed to the sower* and *bread to the eater* in that order. This means that whatever you receive, first take out your seed (tithe) and give it to the Lord. *Don't eat your seed* for it is your seed that unlocks your harvest. When you plant your seed by giving, you should plant it in *faith and obedience*, with the expectation of a harvest, because God is faithful to His word and *the scriptures cannot be broken* (Luke 6:38, John 10:35).

Let a man so consider us, as SERVANTS of Christ and stewards of the mysteries of God. Moreover it is required in stewards that one be found FAITHFUL. – 1 Corinthians 4:1-2

The watchword of Christian service is faithfulness. The Lord's servants (i.e. all true Christians) are expected to serve Him. God never demands too much and He rewards those that seek Him diligently. *The parable of the talents* refers to faithfulness in Christian service (Matt. 25:14-30, Luke 19:11-27). All your abilities come from God (James 1:17).

Talents are opportunities to use our natural and spiritual abilities to serve the Lord. *Time is a precious gift from God: Use it wisely!* The time to serve God is now. You have to invest the opportunities that you have now to serve God now. Don't wait for big opportunities. Your service to the Lord usually starts with little things. In fact, nothing is too small. The little things that you do now will open the door for greater opportunities in the future. It is faithfulness that God rewards, not position. Whatever your daily occupation is, you can use it to honour and glorify God. *You can serve God in your workplace with what you say and what you do*. The eternal status and spiritual maturity of many souls depend on your faithful service to the Lord. Most importantly, your service brings glory to God and an overflow of divine blessings to you.

And whatever you do, do it heartily, as to the Lord and not to men, knowing that from the Lord you will receive the reward of the inheritance; for you serve the Lord Christ. – Colossians 3:23-24

Do you see God as *'harsh, demanding, and unreasonable'*? Are you motivated by fear rather than faith? The servant that refuses to use his talents to serve God is called *'wicked, lazy and worthless'*. What impact can you make for Jesus where you are today? What can you begin to do in your local church, in order to move the work of God forward?

"Do not lay up for yourselves treasures on earth, where moth and rust destroy and where thieves break in and steal; but lay up for yourselves TREASURES IN HEAVEN, where neither moth nor rust destroys and where thieves do not break in and steal. For where your treasure is, there your heart will be also. – Matthew 6:19-21

The steering wheel of Christian service is the Great Commission (Mark 16:14-18). God's plan of *history* is the plan of *redemption*. Therefore, the redemption of souls into the kingdom of Heaven is at the heart of our service to the Lord. All our abilities, gifts, trainings and resources in life are useless if they don't *ultimately contribute* to the plan of redemption. Now is the time to *live life to the fullest*, by using all that you are and all that you have to serve the Lord faithfully.

Don't waste your life. Anything you do in this life that doesn't ultimately contribute to God's purpose (worship) and plan (redemption) is a waste of time and will not count in eternity.

So Jesus answered and said, "Assuredly, I say to you, there is no one who has left house or brothers or sisters or father or mother or wife or children or lands, for My sake and the gospel's, who shall not receive A HUNDREDFOLD NOW in this time—…, with persecutions—and IN THE AGE TO COME, ETERNAL LIFE. – Mark 10:29-30

Beware of Apostasy:

A major feature of the last days in which we live is that the world is now in a state of moral free-fall. Iniquity abounds and the love of many is waxing cold. Due to this atmosphere, the spirit of apostasy is gaining grounds in the church through the increase of *false believers*. The wheat is now mixed with the tares (Matt. 13:24-30). It is not every organisation that calls itself a church that is of Christ, and it is not everyone that attends a genuine church regularly that is a true Christian. Beware of the religious spirit which has to do with only forms, traditions and ceremonies. God is seeking for *true worshippers* (John 4:23-24): those who will worship Him in spirit (with all their heart) and in truth (without hypocrisy).

Hypocrites! Well did Isaiah prophesy about you, saying: 'These people draw near to Me with their mouth, And honor Me with their lips, But their heart is far from Me. And in vain they worship Me, Teaching as doctrines the commandments of men.' – Matthew 15:7-9

A major source of apostasy arises from those who embrace modern man's opinions, ideologies and consensus *as superior to*

Biblical truths. They teach the opinion and psychology of men as the doctrines of God. They use their lips to call the name of God but their hearts are very far from Him.

A good tree cannot bear bad fruit, nor can a bad tree bear good fruit. Every tree that does not bear good fruit is cut down and thrown into the fire. Therefore by their fruits you will know them. NOT EVERYONE who says to Me, 'Lord, Lord,' shall enter the kingdom of heaven, but he who does the will of My Father in heaven.
– Matthew 7:18-21

False believers deny Biblical truths. They are lukewarm: neither hot nor cold. They have the form (look like Christians) but deny the real power (the Lordship of Jesus Christ). They are lovers of pleasure more than lovers of God. *The greatest safeguard against apostasy* is *the written Word of God*. Stay true to the Bible. Stay true to the written Word. Study the Bible and meditate on it often so that you will know the truth for yourself and not be deceived.

**Behold, I am coming quickly! HOLD FAST what
you have, that no one may take your crown.**
– Revelation 3:11

Have you been a false believer? Is Jesus really
your Lord? Do you really believe in the Bible?
Are you like the lukewarm church of the
Laodiceans (Rev. 3:14-22)? It's not too late for
you. All you need do is to repent of Sin,
believe in Jesus Christ and receive Him into
your life as Saviour and Lord. He loves you!

**Behold, I stand at the door and knock. If anyone
hears My voice and opens the door, I will come in
to him and dine with him, and he with Me. To
him who overcomes I will grant to sit with Me on
My throne, as I also overcame and sat down with
My Father on His throne.** – Revelation 3:20-21

We are fast approaching the end of the world.
The rapture is imminent. The antichrist army
is loading. Jesus Christ is coming. What profit
is it to a man if he gains the whole world, and
loses his own soul? What will a man give in
exchange for his soul (Matt. 16:26)?

DOXOLOGY

The Most High is the source of *life infinite*. His purpose in *creation* is *worship*, and His plan in *history* is *redemption*. We are made for worship and we are called to redemption. This is our *design-purpose* in life. The whole of history is His story of redemption. God (*The Father*) wanted a family of worshippers for Himself, so He made mankind (*bride-to-be*) who then fell from grace (*separation*). God became a man (*the Son*) in order to pay the debt of Sin (*bride price*), preach to mankind (*proposal*), and restore the repentant and believing ones unto Himself (*engagement*). Jesus Christ (*the bridegroom*) ascended to Heaven (*suspense*) to prepare the New Jerusalem (*bridal home*) and He is coming back for the true church (*faithful bride*) to rapture her to Heaven (*thriller reunion*), in order to purify and reward her (*bridal gown*) and to be married unto her (*wedding ceremony*) before the Father. They will come back to earth to celebrate their marriage with resurrected saints of other ages (*wedding reception*) and reign together in the millennium (*honeymoon*), after which they enjoy eternity together (*happily ever after*).

And the Spirit and the bride say, "Come!" And let him who hears say, "Come!" And let him who thirsts come. WHOEVER DESIRES, let him take the water of life FREELY. – Revelation 22:17

Jesus Christ is the reason for all creation,
and the risen Lord of all creation.
He is the sacrificial Lamb that was slain,
and the royal Lion with an eternal reign.
He is the King of kings, full of justice and truth,
and the Prince of peace who is faithful and true.
His Name is called 'the Word of God'.
His love endures and His grace is sufficient,
His yoke is easy and His burden is light.
DO YOU KNOW HIM?

Now to the King eternal, immortal, invisible, to God who alone is wise, be honor and glory forever and ever. Amen.
– 1 Timothy 1:17

DECISION

Prayer for Salvation:

Dear God, I come to you today. I acknowledge that I was born with a sinful nature, I have lived in rebellion against You, and I cannot save myself. I believe that your eternal Word came down in human flesh as Jesus Christ, the Son of God. I believe that He died on the cross as the eternal sacrifice for Sin. I repent of Sin and I accept His eternal sacrifice for my sins today. I receive Jesus Christ into my heart as my saviour, and I confess with my mouth that Jesus Christ is my Lord. I choose to trust and obey Him, and to live for Him every day. From now on, I will fulfil my design-purpose of worship as I go through life in faith and obedience to Christ, until I see Him face-to-face. Thank you for saving me. I am now born-again. I'm a child of God and God is my father. I'm a winner. Glory to God! Hallelujah! Amen!

Name:_____ **Date:**_____

ABOUT THE AUTHOR

Dr. Ben AAB Awoseyila is the founding pastor of Healing Springs Church, Basingstoke: a lively, international Pentecostal church with a mission of equipping you to live victoriously.

He obtained B.Sc. (1st Class Honours) in Electronics & Electrical Engineering from OAU, Ile-Ife, Nigeria. He also obtained both M.Sc. (with Distinction) and Ph.D. in Mobile & Satellite Communications from the University of Surrey, Guildford, UK.

Dr. Ben has worked in research and teaching at the University of Surrey for several years. He is passionate about teaching his subject. He is even more passionate about helping people solve their problems, inspiring them to walk with God, and teaching them divine truths for victorious living.

If this book has blessed you, you can share your story and/or send free-will donations to support our mission and/or visit us at Springs Church UK.

Contact: ben_aab@me.com

Donate via Paypal: ben_aab@me.com

Visit Springs: www.HealingSpringsChurch.org